THE POSSIBILITY OF GOD

*A Reconsideration of Religion
in a Technological Society*

For Ken Vaux

Happy we found each other in Edinboro

Hope This is the beginning of many other meetings here.

& Hope our golf is somewhat improved by then

Jim Drane
Aug — 1586

THE POSSIBILITY OF GOD

*A Reconsideration of Religion
in a Technological Society*

JAMES DRANE

1976

LITTLEFIELD, ADAMS & CO.
Totowa, New Jersey

Library of Congress Cataloging in Publication Data

Drane, James F.
　　The Possibility of God

　　(A Littlefield, Adams Quality Paperback No. 321)
　　1.　Man.　2.　Alienation (Social psychology)
3.　Religion and culture.　4.　God.　5.　United States—
Civilization.　I.　Title.
BD450.D67　　　200'.1　　　75–45124
ISBN 0–8226–0321–7

IN LOVING MEMORY OF
MY FATHER JAMES DRANE.

Requescat in pace.

Acknowledgments

As a teacher in a State School my first responsibility is to students and classroom work. The materials in this book were prepared originally for classroom presentation and developed in that context. I am grateful to my students for their patience and prodding.

There is a tendency by authorities to evaluate State School Administrators by production-like standards and consequently the administrators are forced to decide priorities and programs in terms of monetary considerations which do not always coincide with academic values. Chester T. McNerney, President of Edinboro, recently approved money and time to be allocated for research. His decision, made against the current, was an act of academic courage. I am thankful for the help provided by the three hours of released time last semester and for his personal encouragement. Bob Gates, vice-president for Support Services at Edinboro and head of the Edinboro Foundation, provided some needed help in the preparation of the manuscript. Maurice Holloway, chairman of the Philosophy Department at Edinboro, by his support and example has aided in this effort.

With much appreciation, I acknowledge the generosity of my wife Sissy in sharing with the library much of the time we would ordinarily have spent together.

Contents

ix

Foreword

There are a number of ways to communicate the content of the Christian faith—or any faith.

There is the absolute approach, which simply lays it right on the line saying, "Here it is, take it or leave it; if you take it you must accept it completely." Dietrich Bonhoeffer referred to such a position as "the positivism of revelation," and while that phrase does not reveal all, it does suggest the unyielding rigidity that characterizes the approach we are trying to describe.

Another way to communicate one's faith is to say in effect, "Look, you are really a believer already, only you just don't know it. The differences between us are purely semantic. When you say 'man,' you are really saying what I mean when I say 'God.' When you say 'earth,' you are really saying what I mean when I say 'heaven.' When you say 'highest human potential,' you are really saying what I mean when I say 'Jesus.' " When such an approach is taken it is pretty clear that there has been a capitulation by one side or the other, and the suspicion may be entertained that it is the missioner whose faith has collapsed, rather than vice-versa. If the differences are so immaterial, why bother to retain the old language?

Another mode of communication, gradually discredited over recent decades but now making a strong comeback on some of our campuses, is to say, "I know I'm right because it says so in

The Book, and The Book is never wrong." This appeal to authority, which could be the Bible, or the Sayings of Chairman Mao, or the Koran, is something like the absolute approach mentioned above, but it is undergirded by the supreme confidence that there is *A Verse for Everything* and that one is not allowed to question, even for an instant, the *Instant Relevance* of the verse produced. This turns faith into the acceptance of information backed by infallible authority, which may produce momentary comfort in times of doubt but hardly builds up the questioning and probing and pondering attitude that characterizes human existence at its best and most authentic.

Books reflecting the above attitudes are legion. And we can be glad that Professor Drane has not added to their number. To be sure, he is trying "to communicate the content of a faith," and the Christian faith at that. But he is not doing so by bludgeoning, or cringing, or falsely Biblicizing. Nor is he saying, "I've got it all worked out, just listen to me." Instead he is saying, "Let's start where we are, and go on a journey together. You have doubts and questions; so do I. Let's face them honestly. Let's look together at the human condition we share. Let's see if the questions we ask can be made more precise, and if the way we ask them tells us anything about who we really are, and the sort of universe that has produced creatures like ourselves. Let's look at different kinds of answers and sift through them. Some that used to be compelling no longer are. But maybe in our new situation there are some pointers toward meaning that we have either totally ignored or too long neglected. Maybe there are even some new modes of approach, unavailable to our forebears, that can be summoned in our own situation, a situation that forces us to ask questions in ways distinctly different from earlier situations."

Professor Drane then takes us on an ably-conducted excursion through our contemporary world, sharing with us insights that might be pointers toward "the possibility of God." He does not ask us to be fully-trained philosophers or theologians; he supplies those ingredients himself. What he does ask of us is that we be fully open human beings, willing to use our minds—and our hearts—as clearly as possible.

There are no tricks, no sneaky lines of argument that end up with, "Aha! You've come this far, now I've got you hooked." Instead, there is honesty and forthrightness, acknowledgment of problems in the life of faith, as well as recognition of some of the kinds of emptiness of the life of un-faith.

At the end of the day, we all have to do our own believing. But the believing can be done in the context of a community-in-question, and on such a continuing quest it is immensely helpful to have a guide as able as Professor Drane.

ROBERT McAFEE BROWN

Introduction

Throughout its long history, philosophy has had some strange bedfellows. There were times when philosophy was identified with the established political order and other times when it constituted the source of revolutionary sentiment against the establishment. Philosophy at one point was subservient to religion, an *ancilla theologiae* (servant of theology). Later philosophy became the fountainhead of atheism and antireligion. The development of science and technology was supported by philosophical justification. When science became dominant in the West, critical statements about its limitations and dehumanizing influence came from philosophy.

While philosophy has applied its critical apparatus to every aspect of the American Establishment, very little real communication has taken place between those who spend their lives caring for the economic institutions of American culture and those who spend their lives "doing" philosophy. These two worlds rarely overlap. No one ever accused philosophy of concubinage with business, or vice versa. It is presumed that business people have nothing to offer of interest to the philosopher. To the ordinary man in business, on the other hand, whatever it is that philosophers do, it appears far removed from what is referred to in his circles as the "real" world. Some explanation seems warranted of just how these two worlds grew so far apart.

The industrial revolution located the areas of production and commerce outside the home, and far removed from other institutions like the church and the university. There was a time when monastic communities were important economic units, but those remaining have paled into insignificance by even a modest-sized modern industry or business. The university, which was close to the center of things when the center was occupied by politics, law, and theology, also suffered a certain isolation following the turn to industrial production. Once science and technology were converted into industrial production the "real" world became identified with the powerful institutions of business and commerce. What "really" counted happened at work. The "real" world was the world of production, competition, selling, advertising, making money. The home, the church, the university became fringe institutions and fairly well insulated from the productive functions of industrial society.

The home, which was itself once the unit where the basic goods of life were produced, gradually lost its older function and became a private compartment divorced from production. It became a refuge from the "real" world rather than a part of it. Work took place and wealth was developed at "special" places, away from everything else in society. The home became a consumer unit rather than a unit of production and concentrated on activities like child nurture and interpersonal intimacy. What happened in the family had little or no influence on production. Machines ran and men worked no matter what happened at home. The home was supposed to act as a refuge where the working man would recover the strength needed for his role in the world.

The academy, in the sense of the "liberal" subject matters, became just as isolated. The departments of physical science often retained a relationship with industry for the mutual benefit each hoped to derive; utility kept some communication going even where there was little love shared. The humanities or liberal arts, however, were of no use to scientific rationality and the empires it was building. Building, business, production were recreating the world and like God himself assigned the "proper" place for men and women. The latter were to stay home, and prepare a warm, intimate, personal nest for the returning warrior. The former were to go out and do battle in the world of production quotas, sales charts, union demands, etc. Only men who were involved with commercial or industrial enterprises lived in the "real" world. The woman stood alongside the churchman and the professor of literature or philosophy as inhabitants of fringe areas in contemporary life.

Philosophy, especially its humanistic and ethical concerns, has been divorced from what is assumed to be the "real" world. Ethics, as if we needed Watergate to show it, has for some time been either pushed aside as unrealistic or confined to a narrow range of very private affairs. A private man might try being moral in some ways but morality had no place in the world of business and industry (Moral Man vs. Immoral Society). If morality had no place, then neither did a philosophy, or considerations of man and God.

As a person whose life is involved with philosophy, I have no hesitancy in admitting that my profession has been impoverished by its isolation from the marketplace. I am going to assume that there are men involved with business and industry who can entertain the notion that their world has been diminished by its isolation from the humanities. The person entrenched in production or commerce does not have to abandon his whole life style to admit that his image of "manly" is too narrow and his concept of the "real" world is a nineteenth-century construct rather than a perennial intuition into the nature of reality. If those preliminaries are agreed upon, then communication can begin.

As a philosophy teacher I have nothing to say which will in any way claim to make the businessman more productive or more successful. I cannot be strong enough in testifying to my ignorance and incompetence in the so-called "real" world. The few attempts I have made to turn a buck have been miserable failures. There is no doubt in my mind that the most successful business enterprise would under my astute direction plunge precipitously into bankruptcy. My view of the commercial world is strictly that of an outsider. I have no background in either industry or commerce.

I do, however, know people outside my own small academic

community. Business people are my neighbors and friends. My responsibility as a teacher requires that I try to understand even those aspects of reality with which I am not professionally involved. There have been outstanding philosophers who addressed themselves to the condition of contemporary man and I am attempting here to communicate their ideas. My main interest is to make some elements of contemporary philosophy accessible to the person who spends the greater part of his energies in the economic world. Certainly this person is a producer but it is assumed that he is not exhausted by his productive functions. This book is directed to an exploration of "the more" that every man is.

The suggestion that man is a being unexhausted by his daily tasks comes to us from many corners. From unexpected sources comes the suggestion that "the more" that man is, or the "other dimension" of human existence is, religion. Men at the pinnacles of political power and secular success are turning from their important involvements to give themselves over completely to God. Senator Hughes, for example, has decided to dedicate his remaining years to concerns of man's "other life." All over Washington, and around the country, men in politics and business are forming themselves into prayer groups and taking God seriously. These behaviors cannot help arousing curiosity. Is there anything to these religious conversions? Could it be possible that God exists after all? Religion, which had ceased being a real concern for most dedicated practitioners of contemporary life, is making something of a come-back in the seventies.

Religion, like philosophy, has become "strange" to the "real" world of prices and profits. It is, however, being suggested that the more limited concerns of contemporary secular man are in fact limiting and dehumanizing. Religion and philosophy, which have for years been consigned to "limbo," are again being considered. Only the closed-minded antireligious fanatic accuses people like Senator Hughes or his prayer group colleagues of insanity. Rather such people are being listened to, at least in the sense that a new willingness to listen to the humanists or the religious thinkers has developed. There is widespread support for the idea that a broadening of perspectives beyond business brings new vistas and new freedom. This book is a response to the new situation. In the process of considering the situation of the human person in contemporary life (humanistic philosophy) we will look into the question of the possibility of God (humanistic theology). The success of this effort will depend upon whether philosophical and theological concerns can be made real for the busy, pragmatic, secular American.

Part 1

The Human Condition
in Our Culture

There is a point in every life when it must be subjected to serious examination. A young person, for example, brought up in religion, must examine his religious training. He or she is forced by absence from home and different social influences to examine previous relationships to church affiliation and belief. If religious formation and church affiliation are rejected, that is not the end. Some time later the question of Scripture must be looked into. Is the Bible a fairytale or a privileged source of truth? If Scripture is rejected, serious questioning still is not over. Some time before facing death the question of God's existence must be raised. What is true of religion is also true of the culture in which we find ourselves. The critical human person must continually question the quality of life in a culture. Ordinarily, people do not initiate these tough examinations because they are painful. It is always some trauma or crisis that forces man into a questioning mode.

Cultures and civilizations come into crisis just as individual lives do. An individual who constantly experiences negative feelings about the quality of his life will be forced to take a hard look at himself and his style of life. If a culture is bombarded by criticism both from its own people and those outside, then it too

1

will be suspect and questioned. As a matter of fact, this is exactly what is happening. It would be difficult to imagine a person living today who is unaware of all the talk about contemporary culture in crisis. Reactions, bad reactions in fact, are taking place, both in nature and on the part of human beings, to our culture founded on science and technology. Nature very gradually but very persistently has been for some time sending back signals of distress in pollution statistics and other indices of exhaustion. Human beings too in increasing numbers are manifesting, in violence and boredom and mental illness, their own peculiar variety of maladjustment or reaction to the basic institutions of our culture. In the midst of an unprecedented comfort and promise, human beings seem to be losing touch with themselves. Nature is being forced by misuse into impotency, and individual persons are suffering from similar forms of powerlessness and despair. The prevailing mood is one of *crisis*. Doomsday preaching is back in style because in both the natural world and the human world there are events which lend themselves to doomsday interpretations.

The crisis facing contemporary man and his culture is different in many ways from those of other times. When St. John in the Apocalypse talked about an impending disaster he described it as coming from without—i.e., as something imposed upon man. Angels will inflict man and world with disastrous punishment. In this scriptural account life in the sea will be killed. Human beings will be consumed by heat and fire. Rivers will dry up. Thunder, lightning, and earthquake will cause cities to be destroyed. Plagues will visit the ravaged lands. Today we hear similar descriptions of impending doom, but they come from scientists rather than sacred writers. The contemporary forms of annihilation written about are all man's own creation, rather than something imposed upon him from outside: death by thermonuclear heat; the dying of the seas and the life they support; the impending famine; the spoiling of the atmosphere; the diminution of natural resources. The contemporary form of Apocalypse is much more frightening than the scriptural account and we are moving toward it via "progress." It is man's power, might, intelligence, and affluence which threaten to bring on this new destruction. Not confusion but tough-minded planning accompanies every step we take toward Armageddon. Contemporary man's crisis comes not from God but from himself, because the contemporary world is man's own creation.

Chapter 1

American Culture

American culture might suggest to the reader a cluster of activities associated with the mind and with perfection, e.g., the general body of American artistic and intellectual works. Such would be one meaning of the term. In sociology and anthropology, however, the word *culture* has gone through a history of its own and moved away from an identification with ideal works. Now it refers to the whole way of life of a particular people and includes material as well as spiritual elements. We speak now of American culture and also of primitive culture, nonliterary culture, stone-age culture. Once culture was restricted to "elevated" works but now it includes every aspect of the life of a people, including their economic institutions, social and political organization, kinship patterns, language, system of meanings and values. It has been recognized that the mind of man is shaped by all these influences so that there is an intimate relationship between the "ideal" works of art and philosophy and the more mundane dimensions of life. American culture as used here refers to what might be called "high culture" as well as "mass culture." It includes the social, political, and economic institutions as well as the meanings and values which shape the American mind. The closest synonym would be "American way of life."

Crisis Talk

The very idea that America is a culture in crisis will seem improbable to some. From the outside, especially from the perspective of a preindustrial society, America might look like Utopia. People appear to be well fed. They dress fashionably. Their lives are surrounded by every type of mechanical convenience. How could there be trouble? If a nation lacks bread and mechanical conveniences, then acquiring these will likely be identified with fulfillment. Only a people who has for some time enjoyed the materialistic fruits of science and technology can experience their negative aspects. Only the well-fed, well-entertained, affluent American can explain to starving people the need for more and more therapy to continue living. Only a culture which has reached an advanced stage of science-based industrialization can feel the new poverty associated with its wealth.

People on the inside can see through the industrial affluence and scientific sophistication. Our technology cannot hide from us the fact that we are more violent than "primitive" people. The blights of bigotry and hatred have not been removed by our advances but deepened and made uglier. Nihilism and neurosis may escape the view of those who look at us from the perspective of material want, but they do not escape us. We see the many faces of despair which feeds on the strong suspicion that despite our power and wealth we have failed to develop the human potential. Our dwarfed, stunted, diminished humanity is an ugly sight. The Ugly American is now a phenomenon which one does not have to be in Europe to notice. The counterfeit is everywhere with us. So, too, the fake, the moral cripple, and from time to time the man who hates the good and the beautiful which he is unable to achieve. The fruits of scientific industrial society are not all good and we know it. We are rich in things but poor in spirit. Like the people Dostoevski describes in the legend of the grand inquisitor, we seem to have handed over our spiritual heritage for material comforts, and down deep we are miserable.

Reactions to the Crisis

Reaction to the sickness of American culture has been varied. Some, whom William James would classify as "tough-minded," see all difficulty in terms of solvable problems. These types tend to reduce the widespread turmoil to a single cause, like the population explosion or bad organization or too much religion. The tough-minded follow up such an analysis with a solution based on *more technology*. Nothing is ever too serious, because everything can be taken care of with "better technology." Man according to this view has both the know-how and the method for dealing with any and all complaints. Little attention is paid to the fact that human beings in other civilizations literally destroyed themselves by pursuing their technology. (E.g., the Mohenlo-Daro civilization in what is now Pakistan died simply from wearing out its landscape with continued application of technology. The Mayans, too, literally sank into the mud because they had cut all their forests in order to provide power for their technology.) There is a pride, a self-confidence, and an enormous optimism that permeates the tough-minded man. The human animal is confidently in charge of his own situation according to this perspective, and when such a person looks around, it is not disaster he sees but an imminent Utopia. The tough-minded person is usually ignorant of history.

Traditionalists are a different lot and react differently. They ascribe today's crisis situation to a straying from time-honored principles. Not more technology but a return to traditional ways (in either religion, politics, or economics) is their solution. The traditionalist is as strongly drawn to pessimism as the tough-minded person is to optimism. He sees no hope for the dreadful state of affairs today. For him, every attempt to better man's situation is futile. People today are no damn good and the few good ones who constitute the saving remnant (the radical conservatives) seem unable to get anywhere or have any real influence. Here too there is a historical myopia. There have been many cultures which disappeared because they could only look backward. What produced great prosperity and fulfillment at one time need not continue to do so at a later period. In fact the concentration on a past set of successful principles inhibits further development. Spain, for example, is poor today because it was too successful at colonizing. Concentration on that successful pattern (a tradition) led the people to ignore the necessity of developing industry.

Still another very common reaction is the one we usually associate with younger people. The young radical refuses to have anything to do with things as they are. His response to the crisis facing contemporary man and his civilization is to drop out of the system which produced the crisis. He shares the pessimistic assessment of the traditionalist. Neither man nor the earth can be saved. The optimistic engineer to him is a fool. In the midst of crisis the youthful critic heads for a park with a lot of green grass, or in its absence creates one inside his mind with an appropriate dose of grass. Many young people propose to solve the crisis for themselves alone. They set up a new style of life which rejects science and technology. They believe in respecting nature rather than exploiting it. The more adventuresome go off somewhere—far away if possible—and strive to put the new attitudes into operation. The youthful commune constructors or civilization makers seldom are aware of the enormous task of building the human, but they are legion and their foundations are everywhere.

If the three above-mentioned types were able to communicate, they might agree that life today, wherever we are, seems somewhat secondhand. Even the tough-minded engineer, who most likely identifies with the system, in moments of honesty (oftentimes brought on by a mixture of gin and vermouth or some other magic formula) admits to being bored by his life. There is no boredom like that of the man whose life is identified with the projects of a dull business and who seeks relief from his work in a continuing round of "fun cocktail parties." The traditionalist and the radical young agree in their negative assessment of the quality of contemporary life.

Tolstoy put his finger on the high incidence of routine and role playing which people use to cover up the emptiness associated with dehumanized culture, in a moving short story called the *Death of Ivan Illyich*. Ivan was the perfect example of the man living routinely within a system. He was an exemplary Russian officer, who followed faultlessly the expectations of his class and culture. In the midst of a fatal illness, his cultural world collapsed. Suddenly, he saw his life as a series of acted-out roles, similar to countless other lives. He had not been himself, but a standardized copy of what others were or what was expected of him. Ivan experienced his life as alienated and, in his last few remaining days, struggled for authenticity and truly human existence. The story makes its point whether we are part of the Establishment or firmly opposed to it. Authentic human existence is an elusive goal. Life can very easily become merged with what it is not—a world of trinkets, a set of old goals, a new and naive romanticism which makes the truly human synonymous with the completely uncivilized. Everyone has to be careful not to fall into a fictitious role-playing existence. Human life in every culture easily becomes a second-hand existence.

The imminence of death brought to Ivan a light in which he saw both his personal alienation and the dehumanization of the culture he had interiorized. He experienced a type of revelation. Contemporary man's dissatisfaction with his life and the direction of contemporary civilization can provide the occasion for him to reflect and then possibly, like Ivan, catch a glimpse of what being human is all about. Rather than taking refuge in insensitive optimism or maudlin pessimism or undignified flight, he may use the occasion of discomfort within himself and his culture to join Ivan Illyich in searching for a more authentic way to live. The human being that I am is distinct from the roles that I play and the pretense with which I often cover myself. A crisis period is not all bad. It provides an opportunity to become aware of alienation, showy pretense, role playing, dehumanization, and dishonesty. It is even possible that contemporary man, like Ivan, can, after seeing through his culture's distortions, move on to the more positive task of trying to piece together the ingredients of truly human being.

There is then a fourth way of reacting to the crisis situation of contemporary Western man. It requires that he pause and seriously consider his condition. An opening question might be about the very possibility of the human animal with his civilization coming into crisis. What does it mean to say that man is not himself or that he has deprived himself of the conditions for human existence? Animals never suffer such a fate. A squirrel is always a squirrel. A fish is always "himself." There seems to be in the animal kingdom a built-in harmony with nature which is missing in man. How is it possible for man to identify with what he is not; to miss what human life is all about; to build a culture which threatens and diminishes him; to become alienated or estranged from himself in the midst of his own creations? *Alienation* is a word used to describe the mysterious experience of dehumanization. We can begin our reflection on the human condition in contemporary civilization by looking into that term and its use in contemporary thought.

Chapter 2

Alienation

The word *alienation* comes from the Latin *alienare*, which means "to make strange, or to separate" what once was united. The term is used by psychologists, theologians, sociologists, and philosophers, with some slight variation in meaning. In every case, it stands for some kind of disassociation or rupture between man and that which belongs to him essentially. Corresponding to this objective split between the human and that which is necessary for human fulfillment, there goes a subjective disequilibrium which manifests itself in states of mental distress. Wherever the term *alienation* is used, there is presupposed an essence or nature of man which is being violated or a preceding unity which is being destroyed.

Theories of Alienation

For some thinkers, man's nature is seen in terms of an initial unity with his fellow man. Alienation then is understood as separation from depth relationships. For others, man is understood as a complex of capacities and potentialities. Alienation in this case means separation from the actualization of human potential. Karl Marx sees man as a producer, and alienation for him is a separation of man from the fruit of his labor. For religious existentialists, man has a preestablished union with God, and alienation is a separation of man from his creator. In every case, alienation is seen as rupture of a real and normative

11

harmony which must be healed if man is to experience fulfillment. Every theory of man has a corresponding theory of
alienation. To be consistent, a thinker tries not only to outline
what authentic human reality is, but also to show how man may
lose his humanness.

In its extreme form, alienation is psychopathic. In lesser degrees it can become a generalized condition of people throughout a culture. There are ages that reflect specific and peculiar
forms of alienation. Alienation or estrangement is so common
in our age that some philosophers have begun to think of man
as naturally sick or inevitably alienated. Man according to this
view seems plagued by a radical defect which keeps him always
separated from his true self. The basic defect is variously explained. Theological language uses the term original sin, or
original fault. The Judeo-Christian tradition considers every
man to be victimized by a fall which induced disunity and disharmony into human existence. More secular writers prefer to
explain man's radical defect without referring to sin. Marx
thinks of man as victimized by economic exploitation. For Arthur Koestler man's problem is a physiological defect which
occurred in the evolutionary process (e.g., the disconnection between reptile, animal, and rational parts of the brain). Other
thinkers talk of an exaggerated socialization which results from
a human being's long period of dependency upon parents, such
that even the mature person in adult life is unable to realize the
expectations drilled into him during his extended childhood. An
abstract philosophical formulation might express the experiences in terms of man's actual life not being identified with his
being (i.e., his nature or himself). One philosopher (Sartre)
puts it this way: "Man is not what he is," in the sense that
man's true being is the ability to change anything he is at present by a choice. "Man is what he is not," i.e., a conglomerate of
acts and things and moments past, which are far from his true
being.

Man's true being then is variously defined; substantial meaning, depth relationship, sexual delight, identification with nature, creative activity, a union with God, etc. In every case,
where these necessary constituents are absent, there is an objec-

tive break or split from what constitutes man's essential being. Every such break is associated with a state of subjective disequilibrium or a psychological sickness. Sometimes the awareness of disequilibrium and sickness follows from a life crisis (as in the case of Ivan). A cultural crisis, however, rather than a personal one, can also make people aware of alienation in their lives. Sören Kierkegaard, whom some call the father of existentialism, thought that man's depravity is such that even his unhappiness, his shallowness, and his disharmony have to be revealed to him. Otherwise man assumes that the sorry state of affairs in which he lives is natural. If this is true, then a personal or cultural crisis which forces man into awareness of his situation amounts to a necessary revelation.

Becoming Alienated in a Technological Utopia

Man is the only animal capable of being alienated or losing touch with his true self. In the prehuman state, life and being are one. The animal seems to be at one with his surroundings. Cats and dogs do not sit around wondering how they got into this or that condition or dreaming of a new and better way of being. Man developed out of the animal kingdom with all its pre-established adaptations and in the process moved away from its built-in harmony. The emergence of human being is marked by a break with nature that animals are so much at home in.

Human consciousness, by its very structure, splits man off from his surroundings. What man is conscious of is set off over and against him. Language institutionalizes and deepens the rift. As development continues the separation becomes more and more pronounced. The great advances of man, like the development of science, are accompanied by a darker side, a sense of increasing isolation from that which is better known. As science and technology advance, the natural world in which other animals live harmoniously becomes more and more alien. Man lives more in the world which science and technology create (his culture) than in the natural world. Nature is over and against man so that he can use it, control it, change it. The world of man's creation, however, does not always turn out to be a place where he can be at home. Unlike the animal in nature, man often finds himself in a strange and unfriendly cultural world. Even worse, the strange cultural world frequently is taken to be nature. In that case man's feelings of discomfort in a culture become signs of a defect on man's part rather than a cultural deficiency. The way things are in his culture he takes to be the way things have to be. If he is alienated and suffering he concludes that there is something wrong with him. It is much easier to accuse himself than to reform his culture.

There is substantial evidence that the scientific and technological culture in which we live today has in fact become particularly unfriendly to man. For over two centuries our nation has been dedicated to the goals of a technological Utopia. Power, production, things, gadgets, comforts have preoccupied our minds and demanded our life energies. Our dedication to materialistic values has brought a number of rewards. Our standard of life is the highest ever. Technological achievements have in many cases bordered upon the miraculous. We can fly to Europe in three hours. We have landed on the moon. And yet there is abroad a widespread feeling that much of what is essential for humanness is missing from our lives. The goal of still further technological advance does not generate enthusiasm as it once did. Nature is already too much violated. Doubts about technological values and objectives have contributed to a generalized uneasiness about the quality of life in our culture. Our culture is forcing us to reflect upon our lives. Man has built a house but does not feel at home in it.

This feeling is not without foundation. The average American is not prone to radical self-criticism and certainly not to serious criticism of his culture. The way things are, he presumes, is either the way they have always been or the best they can be. This presupposition, however, is now everywhere challenged. If the American is over thirty, or better, over forty, he or she can remember ten or twenty years ago with some clarity, and knows that things were different then. The airline hijackings, for example, have completely changed the character of air travel. He remembers when going on a trip did not mean being searched four and five times a day like a common criminal and having to move around a terminal through a maze of guns, uniforms, tanks, and armored cars. His old neighborhood he might remember as a perfectly safe place to play or walk and now it might be insane to walk along the streets in daylight, let alone at night. There was a time, in the remembered past, which was without political assassinations. Every political administration has had its scandals but never has high-level government been shown to be so full of corruption, intrigue, and dishonesty.

Culture not only is usually presumed to be nature (and natural) but it is usually passed on without too much difficulty to the next generation. Here again there are evident problems. The values and norms, the goals and objectives that generated commitment in other generations are treated by today's younger people with suspicion if not outright rejection. The numbers of young people who simply drop out into some form of life on the fringes of the established culture are unprecedented. Eastern cultures attract many sons and daughters of Western man. There are hundreds of small monasteries now in America, attracting young people into forms of life radically different from the established civilization.

The crucial institutions of our culture were until recently considered to be within the firm grasp of experts, who, armed with computers, were able to adjust the machinery whenever necessary to bring about desired change. Keynesian economists could bring progress out of a period of depression by the rational application of tax reform and business stimulation. Politicians, armed with the best technical advice, could mount programs which would eradicate the worst social ills. One administration might attack poverty and defeat it. In another administration a health care plan would be developed to provide all Americans with the best treatment possible and protect every American against catastrophic illness. But does anyone believe this anymore? Is it not the case that most recently we have been relieved of any assurance that the politico-economic dimensions of our culture are under anyone's control? There is now serious talk about economic catastrophe. The energy crisis has forced upon our production-oriented and growth-minded culture the imminent prospect of declining production and negative growth. These are indicators of a culture in crisis.

Only recently has the man on the street been made aware that there is a price for our materialistic values being demanded of us from the environment. Human beings naturally separate from first nature (the natural world) to produce a culture (a second nature). The construction of the new home uses resources from first nature but these always seemed limitless and man felt free to do anything he was able, to nature and with nature. This foolish attitude now is catching up with him. The culture he created based on industrial production and material gain has only recently shown itself to have a serious negative side—the gradual destruction of first nature. This deleterious side effect threatens to offset all the materialistic advantages of scientific technological creation. Cars are not more important than air. Power to run a mountain of gadgets is not worth the destruction of the earth's water supply. Talk of economic catastrophe is aggravated by simultaneous talk of environmental collapse. Our technological industrial culture has become a threat to the very continuation of human life. We can no longer talk of science and technology creating a wonderful home for human beings. Rather they have become the source of man's alienation.

The Future of Alienated Man

From the very beginning there have been philosophers and theologians voicing grave concern about the adequacy of a materialistic culture. A steady stream of serious criticism of the American culture has come from Catholic writers, of whom Jacques Maritain is the most famous but by no means the only voice. "Material goods are inadequate to the demands of full and authentic humanness." "Pragmatism ignores the spiritual needs of the human being." Those criticisms have been forgotten by most, but a new chorus has recently assembled to sing the same tune.

Soon after World War I chilling doubts about the humanizing possibilities of our industrialized culture were expressed by many influential thinkers. Hemingway talked about it. Existential philosophers all expressed concerns for the future of human life. It would have been inconceivable to the promoters of the eighteenth-century Enlightenment but today the whole program of science, technology, and industrialization is being questioned. Moreover, the suggestion is being made that this culture with all its promise and despite its marvelous accomplishments has shown itself incompatible with human fulfillment. Continuing development, intellectual people are suggesting, means not progress but perdition. It has taken fifty years but finally the message is getting around. "Ordinary" people are becoming concerned about the future of man in our culture. The question is asked whether there can be a future, given a continuation of the disruptions, disorders, darkness, and violence which have recently characterized our man-made world. Is there any light down the road, or does it look increasingly darker? Is there any hope of things improving, or can we look forward only to further deterioration? The alienation from his culture that contemporary man suffers has raised serious questions about authentic human being. Cultural alienation has forced contemporary man to ask about those essential ingredients which cannot be missing without man himself being alienated.

***

The human situation today is judged so critical that radical solutions are being offered by men who have reputations for being serious and balanced thinkers. K. B. Clark, President of the American Psychological Association, is convinced that the only hope for survival of the species is the administration of hard drugs in order to keep man from self-destruction. Clark is joined in this proposal by Arthur Koestler. The first to be drugged would be the political leaders, then criminals, children who misbehave, and finally, all of us. B. F. Skinner, the prominent Harvard psychologist, has proposed an end to freedom and human dignity. According to Skinner, man can meet the threat facing him only if he submits to a behavioral manipulation, which reinforces what will assure his survival. Man has become so threatened by his own hand that serious proposals are being made to turn man into something less than himself (a gentle robot) in order to save him. To save himself in his created culture, man is being asked to give up what we used to understand as truly human existence.

This sounds so strange that some readers will be reminded of science fiction rather than serious suggestions by reputable people. Why such drastic remedies? What evidence is there that man has become so sick and so alienated? Here is a smattering of the evidence submitted:

1. Man has developed into the most aggressive and destructive of all animals. Other animals may kill but they do so for survival and do not kill their own species (rare and temporary exceptions might be cited where there is extreme tension, e.g., not enough space or food for all). Social competition and conflict within the species is settled by combat which is highly ritualistic. Threats and gestures usually end the fight without either animal incurring serious injury. Man is so separated from nature and so alienated from his fellows that he kills his own and does so with gusto. He kills his own, in fact, in scandalously large numbers (hundreds of millions have died violently in our century). Most recently there has been talk of the possibility of genocide. Man persecutes his own and for very little reason. He alone makes war, and any pretext will do. He seems to have lost the ability to be *with* his own. He is increasingly incapable of union, communion, meeting, encounter.

2. Man suffers another dreadful split between emotion and reason. His rational faculties seem estranged from his affective life. Consequently only rarely does he behave according to his beliefs. Nor does he bring his critical faculties into harmony with his emotional life. Thought moves on one level, emotions and feelings on another. Note, for example, the wide contrasts in the behavior of businessmen, political figures, and professional people. They spend their working hours using technological reason which requires the elimination of emotion (Muskie cried and that finished him). Following a certain period of "rational" activity there will be a period of "let-down," when these restrained rational creatures act like damned fools. The cycles of work and let-down differ. Some "relax" every evening, others

on a weekend, still others just once in a while at a convention. No greater contrast can be imagined than that between Wilbur Mills the staid and controlled Chairman of Ways and Means, and Wilbur Mills after work. Rather than being an exception, his life style is that of the majority, only writ large. Rational behavior tends to exclude feelings and emotional behavior tends to be irrational. Man in effect does not "have it all together." Life as a result is very precarious. Following feelings divorced from reason, man does foolish and destructive things. Following reason without feelings, man is turned into a machine or a robot. As the gap between emotion and reason widens human life becomes more threatened.

3. Another cause of concern is the split between man's technological achievement and his ethical development. The power of man's intellect to master the environment has become separated from the power to master himself or improve himself. There were impressive ethical breakthroughs which occurred in the sixth century B.C. like Taoism, Confucianism, and Buddhism. During the same general period great ethical leaders arose among the Jewish people. Some centuries later Christ created a whole new moral option for man based on love, even of enemies. These ethical advances, however, have not gone through the same development as man's Promethean drive to control nature. Ethically, man has become retarded. He has left undeveloped one of his particularly human possibilities: that of doing something with his own self. It is within man's powers to make himself or create himself and to do so according to a model of his own choosing. The increase of power and control over nature, however, came to be at the expense of man's power over himself. The man who reaches for the stars or guides the most sophisticated warheads ethically remains a primitive.[1]

4. Associated with the ethical alienation, perhaps as a species of the generic problem, is the split between man's sexuality and the fuller dimension of human love. Sexuality was one

---

1. Recently televised interviews with those individuals who have their finger on nuclear buttons, or who control enormous arsenals of destruction, leave no doubt about this fact.

aspect of love for the Greeks and not separable from three other important dimensions. Human love included: *eros*—creativity, passion, procreation; *philia*—friendship, concern, communion; *agape*—self-giving, altruism, generosity. Genital sexuality, however, has become split off from all the rest and pursued as the first and only human good (the orgasm as salvation). As physical sex is made to bear the full weight of salvation it becomes strained and distorted. In our "liberated age" sex is more and more available, and yet despite the increase in sexual activity more and more contemporary human beings complain about its being less and less meaningful. Sex divorced from commitment, compassion, intimacy, caring is losing its power to enrich human life. It becomes overburdened with technological demands and pressures to perform. There is evidence that for increasing numbers of people today sex is becoming a cover-up for impotence in the sense of an inability to relate with care, compassion, warmth, commitment. Following liberation from Victorian repression of sexuality we stand in danger of moving into an age when banal, empty, meaningless sex will move man even further from authentic being.

5. We have already commented upon the alienation human beings are suffering from their culture—a split or rupture from societal forces which surround them. Rather than feeling that the institutions of culture (whether economic or political or educational or whatever) are his own and under his direction, man feels that these are beyond him. Contemporary man feels set off over and against both nature and his own created environment. The worker frequently has the experience that the assembly line is his enemy and runs him. Management personnel also experience the industry or business as a threat and feel dominated by it. People from every walk of life feel that the most powerful institutions, those which have most influence over their lives, are beyond their reach and out of their control.

Since cultural institutions form the human world by organizing it into intelligible units, this situation has serious repercussions for the human person. The institutions of a society, besides providing for certain absolute necessities like food, education, etc., organize reality into intelligible units for man and communicate to him a set of meanings. When the institutions become alien to man, split off from him and out of his control, the meaning-giving function of institutions is lost. Instead of ordering things and helping man make sense out of life, cultural institutions produce disorder and isolation, and lead to loss of meaning. Devoid of meaning, man becomes sick and capable of senseless, destructive acts.

6. We have also touched upon the split between man and the natural world. Henry David Thoreau called our attention to it many years ago but only lately has his complaint been heard. Nature, he insisted, is like a mother who is nearby and full of affection, and yet we are too early weaned from her breast. With too much enthusiasm we run from nature to society, from interaction with the natural world to an intercourse with man alone and the institutions he has constructed. More natural people and the many forms of preindustrial existence are looked upon by us as primitive. Their interrelation with wind and rain, sun and stars, hearts and flowers we have abandoned. Split off and separate, we study, control, dominate the natural world but do not see our fate as in any way connected to the physical universe. Despite the efforts of thinkers like Teilhard de Chardin to connect the human to the natural world, contemporary man thinks of himself as split off from nature and pitted against her forces. A stranger to the regular cycles of nature which once gave rhythm and order to life, contemporary man gives serious consideration to the dispiriting suggestion of the absurdity of all existence.

Looking at contemporary man from the above-mentioned perspectives, it is not difficult to understand why he is considered alienated or in crisis. Without agreeing with the radical solutions offered by Koestler, Clark, and others, we can at least see what stands behind their concern. If nothing else, the radical proposals point up the necessity of giving serious attention to the human question, and trying at least to develop a positive philosophy of man.

Before embarking on this task, however, it will be necessary to inquire into still another aspect of the human condition today: contemporary man's myths. Man cannot live life without mythology, and contemporary man is no exception despite his presumption of being scientific and beyond mythology. Contemporary man lives by myths much as men have always done. His problem is not the absence of myth, but its impoverishment. In many ways we are inferior to primitive man because our myths are so much more banal.

Alienating Influence of Contemporary Man's Myths

A critical eye brings to light the fact that, associated with each of the above-mentioned splits within man or between him and a necessary other, is a myth which justifies the rupture. Not only is man separated from that with which he needs to be united, but the separation is held up as a presumed good. The myths of our culture try to convince us that its ways are normal and indeed inevitable. The following are some of the myths contemporary man lives by. In each case the myth accentuates alienation.

The aggressiveness of man is celebrated in the myth of competition. While a degree of competition must be understood as normal for man as it is for every animal, the myth of competition makes aggressiveness and violent struggle the pinnacle of manliness. The myth of competition makes it impossible for those infected by it *to be with* anyone or anything. Everybody and everything is immediately engaged in a struggle. A conversation, a game of golf, a social event, is turned into a competitive affair. The man who lives by the myth of competition is not competitive only in his work. He brings his competitive spirit home from work. He keeps up the competitive mode with his wife, his children, and his neighbors. Even his dreams are full of fighting and wrestling and doing the other in. This myth turns what might be a pleasant tennis match into a death struggle. It poisons even a man's relationships with his family by turning what should be a community into one more field of competition. Such a man might look down in smiling condescension upon primitive people without ever considering the poverty-ridden myths by which he lives his life and the corresponding poverty of his existence.

The split between man's reason and his emotions is deepened and preserved through the myth of rationalism. This myth holds up the ideal of man without emotion, man ruled by reason alone, man so dedicated to order and system that life becomes an unalterable schedule. The myth of rationalism pushes spontaneity and celebration out of contemporary existence, and contributes to the creation of very dull human beings. In reaction, young people live by the opposite myth of irrationalism. Good for them is what makes a person feel good. The object of life is to be high. In the lives of those ruled by the myth of reason, order, pattern, efficiency, and production are idols to which life is sacrificed. In the opposite myth anything that orders, organizes, patterns, or produces is rejected. Sometimes the easiest way to see the myths of the Establishment is to look at the myths of those in radical opposition to it.

The split between technology and ethics endures, thanks to the myth of science. Americans (and perhaps the Russians) operate with the faith that any and every problem can be solved by approaching it with scientific methodology. Technology and science, it is presumed, will save us from any danger. According to this myth, science and technology are pure and good. They are all-powerful and beneficent. The negative sides or ill effects of each are either camouflaged or ignored. If science and technology are shown to be threatening us, or outstripping our ethical capabilities for handling them, then more science and technology presumably will take care of the situation. The human person who interiorizes this myth even looks to science for the solution of the human problem. Once the project of becoming a certain type of person depended on the development of a strong will. Now "proper behavioral conditioning" promises to make man what he ought to be "in a scientific way." Man need no longer make personal efforts on behalf of his own character and personality. Science in the form of controlled behavioral conditioning, it is presumed, will properly modify human behavior and do so without effort on man's part. Will power, because of this myth, has become as passé as sacrifice. The thoroughly contemporary man does not stand out as a person of great inner strength.

The sexuality myth has been most eloquently expressed by the popular "philosopher," Linda Lovelace. In an interview with *Playboy* (September, 1973) she put it very directly: "If you don't have an orgasm daily, you become nervous, very uptight." The corresponding "truth" is that an orgasm a day keeps the doctor away. Human fulfillment is a question of getting enough sex. Ms. Lovelace speaks for many people who spend themselves in pursuit of sexual salvation. Other participants in the same *Playboy* symposium bore witness to belief in the same myth. Genital sexuality, with whomever and in whatever circumstance, is held to be the supreme good. No effort is too much to expend for "a good piece." Swingers in the group interviewed admitted to suffering from repeated social diseases. Sex with unknown partners exposed the believers to all forms of bizarre behavior (one pickup for an orgy got his kick from burning others with cigarettes). Sex divorced from even minimal human concomitants (e.g., knowing the other's name) does not particularly enhance a human life. Technique quickly constitutes another form of repression. Human beings are reduced to genital organs and their functions. Orgasm is both the ultimate victory and the ultimate defeat. Once attained, it pushes the devotee into still another round of activities. Getting the magic orgasm becomes more and more difficult with time. The participants in this myth get as much sex as is humanly possible but do not appear to be particularly happy people.

The split between man and his institutions is bolstered and reinforced by the myths of both Marxism and Romanticism. According to the Marxists, man (in capitalist societies) is inevitably estranged from his production, and from his political systems, his cultural institutions, his laws, as well as his products. Man is condemned to alienation as long as the present economic relations endure. This myth convinces some college-age people that the disassociation of man from the cultural realities surrounding him cannot be overcome without a revolutionary change in the ownership of the means of production. A more generalized American version of the Marxist myth operates among many more young people. The young antiestablishmentarians are new romantics. They believe a version of Rousseau's idea that man's happiness depends upon his success in escaping any cultural association. The farther away from society and its demands, the better. Every cultural involvement is considered corrupting. Sin and culture are identified. Salvation is with the primitive.

Finally, the split between man and nature is sustained by the myth of secularization. According to this myth, the Hebrew faith distinguished itself from Sumerian, Egyptian, and Babylonian religions by standing for a "disenchantment" of nature. In the latter religious systems there was integral relation between man and the cosmos. The Hebrew faith according to this belief separated nature from both man and God. God was above nature and man was set over and distinct from it. Such separateness supposedly justifies man's doing whatever he wants to nature, without fear of God. Nature is not a home for man. Man's link with his animal and cosmic beginnings is totally ruptured. He stands alone. He is not tied to nature in any way. He is its master, its commander, the one called to subdue the earth rather than to care for it. This myth flourished in Protestantism, and especially in the Calvinist tradition. It was built into the American gene package by the Puritan founders and remains one of our uncriticized suppositions. St. Francis and Thoreau are, in the established culture, voices in the urban wilderness. Teilhard de Chardin is a complete unknown.

Each of the above-mentioned myths captures some truth about man, but then exaggerates it out of all proportion. It is true for example that competition increases man's productivity. But it is also true that man is more than a competitor. Man also happens to be a lover. He needs relief from competition as much as he needs to compete.

Who would deny that rationalism has a point? Man must control his emotions. Cool analysis is necessary for survival.

Organization and order eliminate waste and frustration. But man is not just a smoothly running productive machine. His emotions are as important as his calculating ability. Man is also *homo ludens* (man at play). There are times when man must step back from organization and ordering to do the nonproductive thing. Man is the one being who celebrates, and celebration is planned emotional excess.

Science and technology stand for a process of increased control and mastery over nature which in turn contributes to a development of important human capacities (e.g., objective intelligence). The benefits of science and technology are too obvious to mention. But again there is more to being human than can be subsumed within the boundaries of science. When man totally identifies himself with the scientific method he suffers a loss. Science doesn't make poetry, music, or philosophy. Nor does it take the place of ethics or character development. Science can do a lot for man but it cannot live his life without dehumanizing him.

The present emphasis upon sexuality is an understandable reaction to the sexual repressions characteristic of the Victorian period. One does not have to be an orthodox Freudian to appreciate the importance of sexuality. Sublimation of sex can be handled by some people and actually make possible great achievements. These cases, however, are rare. Liberation from Victorian repression has been an overall plus for human beings. The danger in the new myth is paradoxically the same as that of its Victorian counterpart. Sex that is purely genital becomes banal and uninteresting. It leads to a disinterest in sex and sometimes to impotency. Ultimately, like the Victorian myth, it tends to create a-sexual man. In this case as in all the others a bad myth is one which makes one aspect of human existence the whole of human existence. As a result, wholeness loses out.

Marxism too has its point. There is an alienation which takes place in our system between the worker and his products. The product does tend to become the boss. Marxism holds up marvelous Utopian ideals and serves as a tool for criticism of the capitalist system. Beyond that, however, it is another gross exaggeration. Where it becomes established, human beings are reduced to their economic role. It generates totalitarian political systems, with no regard for human dignity. What it criticizes in Western systems, Marxism itself generates to even worse degrees. It too creates dullness, flatness, boredom, and one-dimension men.

Romanticism likewise stresses the important truth that man retains a relationship to nature. Despite the naturalness and inevitability of his cultural creations, man remains a citizen of the natural world. Man's roots are deep in the organic and inorganic kingdoms, and contact with nature remains essential for his fulfillment. It is, however, foolish to affirm man as a being of nature and deny that he is a being of culture. He is both. It is natural for man to put his mark on nature. Whenever there is man, there is a second nature which he creates. Culture isn't evil. It may, however, come to be evil.

This last point is exactly what is stressed in the secularization myth. The human does represent a break with nature but the secular myth exaggerates this phenomenon. There is never a total break. There remains a link, one which it is important for man to cultivate. When he spoils nature, man spoils himself. The more he builds second nature, the more he needs places in first nature, where he can retire and recreate himself. Man cannot develop to his capacity saddled with a view of nature as divine and untouchable. But neither can he be himself without a healthy respect for the structures of nature out of which he developed and to which he remains related.

The myths have their positive and their negative sides, their souls and their demons. Only a continuing critical reflection on them will save man from being dominated by their demonic elements. New myths always have to be in the process of development. Because man lives by myth, some will take the attitude that one set is as good as another. As a matter of fact, however, that can easily be shown to be false. There are good myths and bad myths, humanizing myths and dehumanizing myths. The fact that contemporary man is living by bad popular myths which legitimize and deepen his alienation is not a matter of indifference. In too many crucial areas, our culture gives us a distorted image of what we are as human beings. If we are not clever enough to see through these cultural distortions, and creative enough to improve on them, we are doomed to become an extinct species.

Chapter 3

Psychic Repercussions
of Alienation

Directly related to the alienations enumerated above and the supporting popular myths is the mass of contemporary humanity experiencing varying degrees of mental distress. The mental patients in our culture are legion, and they are by no means limited to those poor unfortunates confined within the walls of mental institutions. If we live in a culture which generates and promotes an objective split between man and what he ought to be for full humanness, then all of us are bound to be affected. Studies of contemporary man which see him as jealous, lonely, helpless, uncertain, unloving, anxious are not describing the mental patient primarily but rather the "man on the street." The alienations characteristic of our culture have their effects on each and every one of us. The psychic repercussions of alienation are inevitable. Sometimes, however, the ill effects are so diabolically illusory that the sufferer in fact needs a revelation to become fully aware of his misery.

Most human beings have to be forced into a reflective mode. Few people today would claim to be happy but most can't begin to figure out what's wrong.[1] Many simply refuse to give atten-

---

1. Cf. Joseph Heller's book, *Something Happened*. In it the "average" man in our culture, despite his successes and affluence, suffers undefinable anxiety, the sense of "something" gone wrong, "something" (very vague) which keeps him from fulfillment.

tion to questions about the quality of their life. Like children they ignore what they feel incapable of handling. In effect they choose the unexamined life. An alternative that is within the capacities of most is to look seriously into the commentaries upon contemporary life coming from many different philosophical and psychological sources. It is not a matter of trying to determine which thinker has *the* true analysis. Rather it is that each perceptive critic provides us with a mirror in which to catch a glimpse of our lives. If we are as a matter of fact alienated and suffering psychically from our situation, the first step toward improvement is a clearer picture of what is wrong.

Emptiness

Practicing psychologists have commented upon the increasing frequency with which people whom one would consider altogether normal, perhaps a friend or neighbor, seek help for a condition they describe as emptiness. It's not that people go around saying to themselves, "I feel empty." Finding a word to identify the uneasy feeling people suffer is itself a difficulty. They feel a vague, nagging dissatisfaction, and this emerges into full consciousness only at privileged moments. At the same time they harbor an unclear but real assumption that human life is meant to be a fulfilling experience. Deficiencies nag at man's spirit.

A man might begin complaining about family problems, perhaps even a breakup with his wife. Dissatisfaction with marriage partners is often complicated by interpersonal problems with colleagues and even neighbors. If his whole situation were clarified for him he could perceive that underneath all his surface trouble is a gnawing sense of incompleteness. A second marriage might have been pursued because it was hoped that this would fill up the life that is "just not right." Underneath the many manifestations of contemporary man's dissatisfaction is an ambiguous sense of loss, which for want of a better term we might call emptiness. In some cases a person feels like a mirror of what is expected of him by others but nothing in himself. He may feel like an empty shell which puts on different shows or plays different roles with different people. In other cases, the complaint is of a gradual loss of goals and desires. "Feeling empty" does not sound very precise or professional but it does come close to describing the overall condition. T. S. Eliot in a poem written around the time of his famous "The Wasteland" says it this way:

> "We are the hollow men
> We are the stuffed men
> Leaning together
> Headpiece filled with straw. Alas!"[1]

David Riesman, the sociologist, put his finger on the same syndrome in his commentary on contemporary American man. He described the man in the suburbs, who gets up at the same time every day to go to the office, to do the same job, eat with the same group, go home at the same time to his 2.3 children, and then go to church on Easter and Christmas. He moves through a routine, an empty existence, till he dies, usually before retirement, either from heart failure brought on by repressed hostility or from boredom. It is his emptiness that propels him at middle age to get involved with "a fresh new thing," or to take up "something exciting" like scuba diving.

What Riesman talked about as the sickness characteristic of the suburban middle class now shows every sign of spreading to all classes. Workers on the assembly line also talk of the emptiness. Studs Turkel's book (*Working*) was full of examples of this same complaint. The so-called lower-class person, however, usually reacts differently. In an automobile factory one worker who piled new cars in uniform racks for shipment simply started dropping cars from his crane for relief. The incidence of workers deliberately disrupting the mechanical routine with all kinds of dysfunctional activity is higher today than industries are willing to admit. Getting high is still another way chosen to offset the empty, helpless feeling associated with assembly line existence. If emptiness were associated with work alone it would be bad enough. But it usually remains unrelieved after work.

---

1. "The Hollow Men," in *Complete Poems and Plays* (New York: Harcourt, Brace and Co., 1952), p. 56.

"Leisure time" is "filled" with stupefying pastimes like watching three NFL games in a row on TV.

Some will say, "Haven't men always felt this way?" I think not. The lives of people from middle- or working-class backgrounds have had their share of negative dimensions in the past but they could not be described as empty. In previous generations people had values, hopes, ideals, basic meaning (usually religious) which gave even a life of hardship substance and solidity. These characteristics now seem in short supply. Formerly there were commonly held aspirations which filled a life; e.g., owning one's own home, getting an education for the children, moving up in the company, holding a responsible office in the community, etc. These were considered very important and saved even a hard life from emptiness. Religious truths, American ideals, ethical standards, national origins, and culture, all these served to give life, even a difficult life, a solidness that is missing today.

This absence of substance and the corresponding experience of emptiness also has something to do with the worst cases of drug addiction in our society. I am not here referring to the young people on drugs, but to those ten million adults who are addicted to alcohol. Psychologically people drink because alcohol is a central nervous system depressant. It relieves tensions and curbs anxieties. It both produces good feelings and covers up bad ones. Although there are many particular reasons why people drink to excess it is common for males to drink in order to *feel strong*, i.e., to overcome the sense of emptiness. Women also gain a *fuller* feeling, in the sense of feeling more womanly, more attractive, more worthwhile. It would be a gross over-simplification to reduce the enormous epidemic of alcoholism in our country to one single psychological cause, but research on the problem shows up instance after instance of a person taking refuge in alcohol from the symptoms we have subsumed under the general term of *emptiness*.

Human nature is a complex of capabilities and powers which, if not actualized, stagnate, thereby creating the sense of loss. If this discomfort is not remedied in a healthy way by making something of oneself, then very often the symptoms are erased with the help of some drug. Almost every society has used some form of intoxicant but the instance of excessive and crippling alcohol intoxication in our time points to the serious psychic problems of contemporary man.[1] Because the feeling of emptiness is related psychologically to a loss of capability and power, particularly plagued by it are middle-aged persons. Forty years of age or thereabouts often brings a realization of impending impotency. Menopause is associated with the awareness that one cannot go any further, or climb any higher, or become any prettier, or change the rather widely held opinion others have of one. Power is strong feelings and desires which enable a person to achieve. Loss of strong feelings and desires is part of emptiness. Unless new directions and enthusiasm and projects can be developed in middle age, alcohol most likely will be used to provide a temporary and artificial fullness.

Loneliness

Another symptom which vies with emptiness in the frequency with which it is cited as the principal complaint in offices of psychologists, priests, or ministers is loneliness. When men lived in small tribal communities or belonged to the disappearing extended family it was almost hard to be lonely. There were always people around. When some one person was in need, the "family" gathered around. There were always a few uncles besides the father to help bring a boy to manhood. There were always brothers, sisters, brothers- and sisters-in-law, cousins, and aunts to keep a person from the suffering of being alone. Families lived close to one another. Neighborhoods were very permanent. There was little chance of being left out, or isolated, or cut off from the rest.

Our technological civilization has ushered in the nuclear rather than the extended family. It has created a small, highly

---

1. It is possible that only the Soviet Union, the second industrial power in the world, has a greater problem with alcoholism. Is there some relationship between man formed by an industrialized society and the sense of loss or emptiness?

mobile family unit lodged in great urban centers. In this new situation not only is it easy to feel isolated or cut off but such has actually become the common plight of millions. One need not be particularly perceptive to see the parallels between the primitive men who, when separated from the rest, banged together objects, lighted fires, or shouted in the forest, and the city crowds seeking out the night lights and loud noises. Both are reacting to the fear of loneliness. City people feel loneliness and fear it, perhaps more than the solitary primitive in the forest. Alone, the human person is deprived of the others' reactions and correspondingly of a sense of self. In total isolation man would no longer be able to distinguish between the world outside and the interior world of his own subjectivity. We are all somewhat like blind people who pick our way through the world by touching others. When those others are missing our sense of reality starts to slip away.

There is an unmistakable relationship between people who live in a world of things and the sense of being cut off and lonely. Every relationship with things is partial for man. What he does to things and with things he never does with the whole of his being. Relationship with things is utilitarian and definitionally impersonal. Intimacy and warmth are understandably missing. The relationship of a person to the tools which surround him and make his world is characterized by distance and aloofness. This·is necessary for the proper manipulation of tools. Since human persons never get fully involved with or committed to a tool, the man who primarily relates to things gradually loses the capacity for full involvement or commitment. He might achieve brilliant manipulation of objects but at the same time his world takes on a coldness and lack of resonance. Even other human beings tend to become tools to be used and manipulated. The world distinguishes itself by an absence of warmth and intimacy. There is a connection then between contemporary man's world of advanced technology and the corresponding experience of loneliness. Technological man may dominate the earth with his tools but he soon finds out that this victory at the cost of a capacity for warm, intimate human relationships is pyrrhic.

Our films, poets, philosophers, psychiatrists, artists, all attest to the sad fact that contemporary man has many things and yet is plagued by an estrangement from his fellows. "Look at all the lonely people, where do they all come from?" There are so many lonely people that the pleasure of being alone or withdrawing for a while has almost disappeared in our time. Solitude is no longer a virtue. It is a threat and a source of fear. Because men today have lost the knack of being together, they are afraid of being alone. Many a marriage continues despite the absence of deep, warm feelings because the loss of that one other amounts to facing a life of total emptiness or total loneliness.

The intimacy of the first nine months and subsequently the union with family founds a strong social dimension in the human animal. The absence of intimacy and depth relationships is not just an inconvenience; it is an alienation from what man needs to be human. The subjective psychological side of this alienation we call loneliness and it is not a petty or a childish disorder. Either we have deep, warm relationships or we wither. Willy Loman in the play *Death of a Salesman* was a man with superficial relationships. He thought he could substitute popularity for more substantial relationships. He told his son, "Be well liked and you'll never want." But he was wrong. Willy Loman is a monument to the tragedy of loneliness.

The Beatles in their day were poets, who saw a lot more than meets the less talented eye. They saw the lonely people and they asked, "Where do they all come from?" But the Beatles had no answer to their own question. Rather they joined others making loud noises and getting high. Like primitive tribesmen they shouted and clanged to keep away the pain of loneliness. Older people join an unending pilgrimage to cocktail parties and social gatherings. Distraction, however, is not enough. Making money isn't going to do it. Having a lot of parties isn't any kind of answer. Creeping back into the womb won't work. In order to survive, the human being must be able to generate deep, meaningful human relationships. Otherwise he'll be a hollow man, a stuffed man, leaning together, filled with straw.

Apathy

Still another way to describe the subjective side of contemporary man's alienation is to use the term *apathy*. Reality understood as the social reality or the culture has become a giant threat. Especially people in big cities sense the world in which they live as a jungle. One way of handling the constant fear is the repression of feeling. The threatened person simply turns off as much of reality as possible. He adopts a noninvolved, noncaring, unfeeling attitude that is sometimes described as "cool." Very often "coolness" is a cover for apathy which is as much a human disorder as emptiness or loneliness.

Personally I notice a certain coolness or aloofness descending upon me when I enter New York. The New Yorkers themselves are cool and detached and the visitor quickly takes on a similar mood. The outside world is so overwhelming, so powerful, so full of alien noises and forces that withdrawal becomes the only way of handling the threat. So much is going on beyond one's control that people retreat or put up a wall around themselves. A visit to the subway during rush hour is an impressive experience for outsiders. The wildest and most unusual scenes, ones which stop the visitor in his tracks or bug out his eyes, are simply ignored by the native city dwellers. Apathy becomes a way of life in the big city.

In the face of too much alien reality, the human animal withdraws, loses interest, and quits trying. He abandons any effort to change things by his own efforts. The detached, aloof, superior acting person is oftentimes one who is suffering from apathy. The cool, detached exterior is frequently a cover for violent feelings. Apathy and violence are closely related. The person who retreats into apathy as a defense against being manipulated, or overwhelmed by a threatening exterior, is likely in a moment of weakness to explode into violence. The apathetic person tends to feel unloved, and even mild criticism may be taken as an attack or a humiliation. Being cool is an artificial response and when the facade falls, fury is unleashed. A society characterized by detachment and aloofness is generally not a safe place to live.

Apathy and submerged violence are, however, not confined to the city. One runs across the same situation on the college campus today. Students feel threatened by a big institutional other. One way of handling the situation is simply to retreat to one's own little garden to let the rest of the big outside go to hell. It is difficult today to get the typical college students to feel strongly about anything. Elections, world events, economic crises, nothing seems able to generate excitement or involvement. Speakers come to campus with what might seem to be very stimulating topics, but there is no way of telling how few students will show up. The only sure crowds on campus come to sit and listen to a rock concert. Perhaps feeling capacity has descended to the point where only the loudest possible sounds generate a reaction.

A personal experience pointed up this development to me in a rather shocking way. During a summer course I was teaching last year, a tragedy occurred on campus. While swimming in the campus lake, one student suddenly turned up missing. A number of others started looking around the area where he had been seen. It was some time before someone found him on the bottom and dragged him out. An ambulance was called and frantic efforts were made by the volunteers to revive the young man. These failed and after about a half hour or so, he was pronounced dead. A young man's life was absurdly snuffed out in the midst of preparation for a career. Parents and family who loved him were unexpectedly crushed by his sudden death. A human life which at one moment was strong, vigorous, full of life, in the next was a shocking, limp, motionless corpse. Such things happen at one time or another in every community. What was strange about this case was the reaction of the surviving students.

I talked to a number of them after the incident and was myself shocked by the consistency with which they confessed to have experienced no feeling whatsoever regarding the tragedy. It was as if that particular reality had been rejected. The students told me they just simply went back to the activities of playing and swimming. Nothing more was said. No comments were exchanged. No reflections were caused by the incident. I still think that this must have been an unusual group I interviewed, but the fact remains that the reported reaction was shared by everyone I spoke to. Students today are in fact more apathetic, and their apathy extends beyond the official institutional life of the campus. It has spread even to personal relationships and personal tragedy.

One has to be cautious in extrapolating from particular events. But the many incidents reported of rapes, beatings, murders, witnessed by many who "just didn't want to get involved," do point to the same pervasive apathy or loss of feeling. Those who perform these acts are schizoid, lacking feeling capacity to a psychotic degree. Those who witness the acts without response are not far behind. People have lost contact with other people and with the cultural realities which surround them. Separated from these they become afraid and withdraw. Etymologically, apathy is *a pathos*, a withdrawal from feeling. It is a studied practice of being unconcerned and unmoved. If, however, it continues for any length of time, it becomes a character trait. Gradually the withdrawal from the outside and from others leads to a withdrawal even from one's own life. Apathy becomes a form of personal death.

In the sixties cultural and social events tended to pull people into involvements. The war in Vietnam was a symbol of everything wrong with society, and many who suffered dissatisfaction found a ready point around which to rally. It was easy to get involved. One experience with a big rally or a picket line strengthened the commitment and drew the participant deeper into a movement. A symbol draws people together and generates action. The opposite of symbolic is diabolic. The diabolic is what pulls apart and enervates. Without symbol creating unity and involvement, people have slipped into diabolic apathy. The movements (protests, upheavals, crusades) which defined the decade of the sixties seem to have disappeared. The war, which rallied people and stimulated them to act, has been removed and the socio-political activity it generated has disappeared. Not long ago there was much concern about finding ways to reconcile the many warring factions within the country. In a very short time there seems to be nothing left to reconcile. College students are quiet. People seem to be asleep. Apathy seems to have "solved" the problems.

Not even the Watergate disclosures of high-level corruption and conspiracy to undermine the American political system were able to arouse the average person. The liberal and radical leaders of the sixties have been unable to regroup. Their old constituencies appear exhausted. Those who led the protests in the sixties were caught without a viable alternative in the seventies and people have abandoned them. The official myth is that things are getting better. People, we are told, have abandoned movements and protests in order to join with the serious-minded to solve our problems. Contemporary man, we are assured, has moved beyond symbols and myths. The scientific experts in the computer-rich think-tanks are planning for every contingency and programming our future. But this is a new myth that no one can really believe.

The feelings of emptiness, loneliness, and apathy are all connected. One experience gradually leads to the other. Human beings cannot stand being empty and lonely for long. Either man finds a project or he stagnates. Either he cranks up his vital energies or he slides into violence or apathy. Some people choose violence as a way of generating feeling and avoiding the loss of affective life altogether. There are contemporary forms of psychoses and neuroses which become the only ways some people have to avoid an even worse disaster. The horror flicks, the morbid, the insanely cruel, the animalistic, the diabolic become the last resort for alienated and dehumanized people.

It is time now to move from a description of contemporary man's alienation and psychic discomfort to a more positive effort, that is, to put together an affirmative philosophy of man. The condition of man today, especially his suffering, points beyond itself to the way things ought to be for man. It is one thing to look at the condition of contemporary man and survey its many points of distress. It is another thing entirely to use these insights to develop a unified theory of man which explains not only why he suffers, but also how he might better handle the delicate human enterprise. Finding the right conceptual categories to communicate a theory of humanness which makes sense to those who are not professional philosophers or psychologists will be the concern of the section which follows.

Part 2

The Structure of Human Existence

The first thing that strikes any serious student of the human condition is a paradox. On the one hand, man is the lord of the universe, a user of its resources, a manipulator of its power. On the other hand, he is the slave of the universe, a feeble pawn in the hands of powerful natural forces which threaten him at any moment with extinction. Man, the lord, is the only creature who knows reality in the sense of being able to name its many elements and organize them into a whole which he calls cosmos or world. Man also judges what he knows. He alone gives value and arranges reality into hierarchies of good and evil. The peculiar form of knowing called science has enabled man to control and manipulate the world so that he has literally taken possession of it.

If man is lord of the world, he is not its creator. His control is never total. In fact the goal of total domination is one that always eludes him. The Promethean urge has a diabolic side. At the very moment when reality is about to be delivered into his hands, man seems to weaken and fall a helpless victim either to that which he would make subservient or to himself. For example, the backlash of nature we witness today reminds man that he is not total master. In fact he stands in danger of being destroyed by a violated and unbalanced environment. Man's lack, his weakness, his helplessness is never more evident than in eras of greatest human power.

One way to express this awareness of man's paradoxical situation is to say that man is simultaneously the presence of being and nonbeing. Man is at one and the same time *some* thing and *no* thing. Man *has* something and *lacks* something. The lack, the absence, the nonbeing is as much a part of man as his power, his presence, and his substantiality. Without nonbeing there would be no movement, no life in man. He strives and struggles for that which is not yet. Nonbeing is both within him and outside him. To be a man is to struggle to bring something into being which before was not. Man works to overcome deficiencies in the world and he works to overcome deficiencies in himself. Since the combination of being and nonbeing is absolute, human life in the world is inevitably a place of struggle. To be a man is to be a unity of being and nonbeing, of power and impotence, of good and evil, and then to experience both the glories and the ignominies of such a situation.

The many forms of alienation we described in Part 1 were traced to an absence of what man ought to be. Each was a form of lack, impotence, or nonbeing. An individual might be at once a vital, creative person and one who senses an absence of vitality and creativity. Even in the act of creating, an artist senses what is not there—i.e., he is aware of the deficiencies and limitations of his activity. The same is true of every human experience. Even peak experiences like love, after the initial glow of ecstasy, show their lack, their negative side, the absence which founds the need for continual struggle and improvement. The many forms of human anxiety we have described (emptiness, loneliness, apathy) are founded upon the reality of absence, lack, or nonbeing in man's life. *Anxiety* is a general term which connotes an awareness of nonbeing; an awareness, however subtle, of something missing. Because nonbeing is a part of the human condition, so too is some form and degree of anxiety. If nonbeing is mixed with being in man, anxiety, the psychological expression of nonbeing, is always part of human existence.

The human being is anxious because he is not fullness of being. Man, despite his illusions of greatness, is not God. Death, the ultimate nonbeing, always hovers over his efforts to deify himself and plays a part in all man's fears and anxiety. The most basic anxiety concerns not being able to preserve one's self or to keep one's self together in the face of threats. From this basic anxiety there is no escape. All the other forms of anxiety we discussed above are related to the ultimate anxiety of death. Loneliness, emptiness, apathy are each a lesser form of dying and each would lose its sting if man were not infected with the worm of death.

If nonbeing in this and many other forms is always present, then we can ask about the being with which these lacks coexist and on which they depend. What is the positive structure of man? Each example of nonbeing, or deficiency, points to a corresponding positive reality. We catch some glimpse of the being of man by viewing his nonbeing. The fact that man is such and such a being makes it possible for him to suffer such and such a lack.

Chapter 4

Man's Physical Dimension

"To be [a man] is to be in the world." That statement sounds innocent enough. It may even sound simplistic or too obvious to warrant comment. And yet man's being in the world is a deep mystery and an enduring source of reflection. Because man is a physical being in a physical world he bears a relationship to everything and shares the conditions of all living beings. He needs a place to be and a time to be. He needs warmth, and food, and air. He needs light, and rest, and other bodies. The material base of human life is both a source of support and a source of insecurity. At any moment one of the constituent elements may be removed. Man is surrounded on every side by forces so powerful and destructive that no defense can save him. Being in the world terrifies man. On the other hand, the same world provides him with abundance of light, heat, beauty, fruit, grain, meat, and millions of his fellows. Being in the world both delights man and terrifies him. To be in the world is to be caught in a paradox which calls out for thought. Man's worldly being drives him to seek a security which he never finds. He wants to have a fixed place in the world and nowhere is there stability; everywhere there is motion, change, and threat. Life is short. Man is unsure of his origin and even more unsure of what awaits him after death. To say that man is physical or that he is a being in the world is both simple and profound. Not only is man in the world but the world lives and dies through him. Man's being in the world brings both the world and himself to reflection.

Space and Time

Each aspect of man's higher being has its foundation in the physical, especially in his peculiar biology. A striking cortical development of the brain accompanied the emergence of *homo sapiens*. This greatly diminished the instinctual determination which characterizes the rest of the animal kingdom. Man became capable of understanding his world. Consequently he relied more and more on this new capacity, and less and less on a pregiven adjustment dictated by the instincts. Man came to be aware not only of his world but also of himself. Self-awareness —reflected in the use of *I* or *me*, and in attempts to call attention to one's ego—has been both a blessing and a source of anxiety. Awareness extends to the shortness of life and the inevitability of death. Man is the animal with both a consciousness and a concern about death. Burial rites are one of the distinguishing features of *homo sapiens*.

Man is aware of a development which brings him from stage to stage, through childhood to adolescence, maturity, old age. The physical structure of human existence means that man is in time. There is, however, no necessity that he continue in time. Temporal existence, our being here at this moment, is not accompanied by the necessity that we continue in being to the next moment. Temporal existence is contingent and not necessary. There was no necessity that we began existence at a certain time (it could have been delayed a night or a week or forever). Even more obvious is the fact that life once begun will not keep going. Life is not synonymous with necessity. It will end and there is no way of being certain when. Our temporality, our being in time, is filled with contingency and uncertainty. This is one form of the nonbeing associated with physical being.

When we stop running away from this fact and face it, it causes us discomfort. If we feel ill for any extended time we become acutely aware of our contingency. We begin to think that we are losing our grip on life. Serious sickness reminds us of our temporality. Accidents, if survived, are powerful reminders of just how contingent and uncertain is our human existence.

Each of these experiences of our physical dimension is associated with anxiety.

What we have said about man in time is equally true about man in space. Our physical dimension requires that we be in space but not in any certain space. We are here now. This is the place we occupy and from which we look at the other objects and people around us. But there is no necessity that we be here. Our being here is contingent. It is contingent upon a hundred different factors, no one of which is necessary. You, my reader, could very well be somewhere else. Working people in America today do not need to be convinced of this aspect of existence. "Here today, gone tomorrow"—that a person supporting himself or his family understands all too well. We would like to make our place certain and secure just as we would like to make our time certain and secure, but we cannot. We humans live a pleasurable and precarious existence. Our lives are combinations of physical delight and terror, and the foundation of both is our physical existence.

Suffering, Death, Courage

The ultimate anxiety associated with our physicalness concerns death. Only because man is radically contingent, i.e., condemned not to continue in existence but to die, is there a sting to the relative contingencies of sickness, accident, transfer, or firing. Sickness or loss of job is a threat and a source of anxiety only because man dies. If there were no death, these threats would lose their sting. The ultimate physical nonbeing of death is by far the toughest to face. The difficulty is compounded by the fact that man must face death surrounded by an ignorance of what may happen afterwards. It's one thing to have to die—it's another not to be sure what death holds in store for us. Sickness and loneliness are relative threats. Death is the absolute threat. Both relative and absolute threats are inevitably associated with the structure of man. They are the negative side of his physicalness. So too then is the anxiety which these generate associated with the very structure of human existence.

There are ways that man can fight the nonbeing which dwells within him. For example, he can hustle. He can try to guarantee his place. He can struggle to make sure he is not displaced. He can expend his full energy to make his place secure and necessary. The threats which originate from man's being in space and time can be resisted with great imagination. Man can take care of himself, exercise regularly, even take Geritol in order to hold back the temporal process. Struggle as he may, however, there is no ultimate victory. There are no real guarantees. Inevitably, the nonbeing which inhabits the being of man will emerge and conquer. There is no final security. No amount of effort and no amount of good health will ultimately prevail.

Ordinarily people do not bother to look seriously into the implications of being in space and time. These very words seem abstract and obscure. Some might be interested in a theory of space and time, but not in inquiring about the deeper personal implications. Time, for most people, means nothing more than a vague realization that we have already been (a past), and that there are certain things to which we look forward (a future). The present becomes a fleeting moment between these other poles. Each moment pushes the other into the past. Life is a series of passing "nows." Ordinarily, contemporary man tries to increase the pleasant moments, decrease the unpleasant ones, and generally avoid disturbing thoughts of a possible deeper meaning to his condition.

There are, however, other ways of looking at man's physical being. Being in time, for instance, means that we are unfinished beings. Man is a being who lives in possibilities and projects which are not yet. Of necessity he himself is "not yet," or still "to be done." And yet there is no completing man's projects or his possibilities because of the inevitable time limitation. Not only is man unfinished but he is condemned to remain unfinished. Death will always catch him short. To be human is to be "on the way" and at some point along that way is the abyss of death which will cut short possibilities and projects. Death condemns man to be unfinished. It means he will never be full or complete.

"To stand up" against death means to approach the dreadful

abyss which belongs to human existence without coming un-stuck. It means to realize more than the meaning of the abstract proposition, "All men must die." Rather it involves experienc-ing one's own personal nothingness without fainting. Some try to avoid this challenge by taking a "factual" view of death. "Even man must die." "Death is a fact of life." Relief is possi-ble with such an attitude but only at the expense of a distortion. The fact that every man must die is true but neither interesting nor relevant to a personal life. The "real fact" is that life is not impersonal but personal. It is always my life or your life. "Everyman" doesn't die. You die and I die. The human being which we are is a being heading toward a particular and per-sonal death. "The end" will be the end of our projects, possibili-ties, and relationships. It is a particular individual life that is cut off, or falls into nothingness. That is the "real fact" and if faced cannot help causing an uncomfortable mood. To discover death is to discover personal limit, finiteness, unfinishedness.

Facing up to the human means facing up to the fear and anxiety caused by the "fact" of my personal death. Rather than "thinking death away" or "arguing it away" the courageous man stands up and faces it. He does not spend his life running away or covering over the fact of his death. He is neither ab-sorbed nor immobilized by his death, but he does expect it. He realizes that his personal death puts an end to his individual life with its possibilities and projects. There is an end to him and to them. And yet the courageous man withstands. He suffers anx-iety but does not succumb to it. Rather he goes on living and acting and hoping.

Understanding what it means to be physical, to be in space and time, puts a man into contact with his being. It sheds light on his life and raises questions about its meaning. Every man can identify with Socrates as he thinks about the meaning of dying. Death confrontation gives a new seriousness to life as it did in the case of Albert Camus. And finally it gives men direc-tion and commitment as it did for Paul and Luther. Life has to be lived as it is. Illusions and escapes are failures of courage. By understanding death as one's own rather than as some imper-sonal "fact" of life, man moves away from unreality and cowardliness. He moves toward reality and health. Courage is what makes this movement possible. The only emotionally healthy response to the human condition is to face it with courage.

Courage is the power to affirm oneself—to keep together—to go on building and being despite the threat which inhabits the human condition. Without courage the nonbeing which we are overcomes us and determines our existence. Young people who recognize the threat of death in the stockpile of awesome weapons that surround us today and then freak out on drugs are examples of a failure of courage. So are the neurotics in the Establishment who become health nuts or permit no mention of death in their presence. William Randolph Hearst, the great newspaper tycoon, was an example of the latter reaction. He tried through power and wealth to build a wall between himself and the human condition. A fairyland world was constructed by his orders where the mention of death was prohibited and everything was arranged to create the illusion that life would never end. Hearst in his latter years showed himself a weakling and a fool. Given the human reality, the only alternative to courage is a flight from reality. Running away, however, is never a solution. It is rather a form of weakness. Minor forms of this weakness we call neurosis. When the weakness becomes acute we call it psychosis or just plain insanity.

This anxiety which man suffers because of his physical makeup precedes choice and is independent of our control. The way we handle this anxiety, however, is very much within our decision-making power, and courage is the key to proper handling. Courage does not remove anxiety since anxiety is the inner side of man's physical condition. It does, however, provide the strength to face anxiety. Courage is the power to keep oneself together even in the face of the threat of nonbeing. Courage is self-affirmation. It is the power to face nonbeing, death, disease, or whatever, without falling apart. It is the power to keep going, despite the negativity in the human condition. It is the refusal to give up. Courage is the stuff of human life in the sense that it is what keeps the human self together when anxiety would tempt us to crumble.

Courage then is a key to good health. Its absence is always a form of sickness. If man does not affirm himself, he has to hide somewhere. Either he reduces the reality which threatens, or he reduces himself. Hearst tried to reduce reality. He commanded that death not be mentioned. He eliminated the obituary page. He took extraordinary precautions against sickness. In other words, he tried to reduce reality to where he could handle it. He tried to make his subjective anxiety dictate the objective reality, and this is the root of all insanity. Other people retire to castles or fortresses within the mind and abandon the objective reality entirely. They live in dream worlds, inaccessible even to the psychiatrist. All these ploys and substitutes for courage are futile. The fact is that to be a man is to be a contingent physical being who dies.

If it is futile to try escaping from the radical contingency of human existence; it is positively beneficial to face this fact squarely. Philosophers from Plato to Heidegger have called attention to the relationship between facing death in a personal, concrete way and living an authentic human life. Man cannot begin to appropriate his life until he experiences it as death-bound. The death experience, internalized and personalized, throws light on the reality of human life and makes possible a new grasp of human existence. (No one comes away from a brush with death the same person.) Rather than letting life slip away in superficial trivialities man returns from the death experience with not only a new appreciation of life but a firm resolve to live it more intensely. Socrates did his best philosophizing in anticipation of the fatal hemlock. In the face of death he understood more clearly. Camus at age seventeen returned from a bout with tuberculosis hardly recognizable as the same person. He turned his life toward a serious pursuit of human questions. The death experience of Paul and Luther changed both these men and consequently the whole Christian world. Paradoxically, running away from death is itself a form of dying. Facing death in a realistic and individualized way, on the other hand, is the beginning of life.

Chapter 5

Man, the Meaning Monster

It is characteristic of contemporary philosophy and psychology to see man only in his physical dimension. The development of contemporary science with its emphasis on measurement was so successful that every other discipline tried to imitate its methodology. What once was political philosophy or philosophy of culture is now practiced under the tag of social science. The scientific method or some version of it is applied to every area of inquiry. As a thoroughgoing scientific culture, America witnesses both to the advantages and disadvantages of such an approach.

What once was called the philosophy of man became the science of human behavior. Freud, for example, found philosophy too abstract and insisted upon approaching the human psyche as a scientist. He assumed that man was physical and nothing more. Every claim he made was supported, he thought, by some type of empirical evidence. He couldn't measure the Oedipus complex or show the functioning of repression in mathematical formulas but he assumed that each of these concepts could be shown to exist in people's behavior. The Harvard psychologist Skinner takes the scientific approach a step further. He too assumes that man is just physical and insists on even more rigorous empirical verification for any acceptable proposition about human life. Man is studied from "the outside" and outside forces or stimuli are the tools of therapy. The more rigorous American "scientists" reject Freud's ideas as unscientific and mythological.

In defense of Freud it can be said that a great deal of what he thought about man was insightful and remains valid even in the absence of strict scientific verification (e.g., his theory of the unconscious). In criticism of Freud it must be pointed out that he never came to appreciate the relationship between what he "found" or thought he found about the human being and the methods he employed in his search. If your tools of inquiry are unsophisticated measuring sticks you are going to get unsophisticated measurements. All findings are relative to the methods employed. When contemporary students of man undertook to understand man with a methodology which was applicable only to the physical, they certainly were going to get back only physical data. Every aspect of human life that does not appear as physical or follow physical laws is by definition excluded by the methodology. The image of man developed by such thinkers has become more and more impoverished, deterministic, and machinelike.

Freud gave very little attention to the meaning systems of his patients, concentrating rather on their physical drives and instincts. He spoke of confining himself to the ground floor and basement of the edifice. So confined by his methodology, what went on in the upper floors escaped him. As the psychiatrist Victor Frankl was later to discover, the presence or absence of a meaning system, the beliefs a person lives by, are more important for mental health than physical factors like a balanced sex life. Freud was hampered by an uncritical acceptance of his methodology. Behaviorists who use a stimulus-response model for investigating man and then deny the relevance of experience which falls outside their methodology are victims of an even more crippling blindness.

Spirituality and Symbols

Only the most flat-footed materialists consider man to be exhausted by the physical. There are other dimensions of human existence which are not reducible to physical parts, and for want of a better term, we can refer to these as spiritual. If man must act courageously in the face of threats originating from his physicalness, he must do likewise in the spiritual realm. Spiritual self-affirmation is standing firm or keeping one-self together in the face of threats to the meanings in which man lives. Before discussing this spiritual type of courage we have to say a few words about spirituality in general and its role in human life.

Neither man nor the reality with which he interacts is purely physical. Man is not an object in a world with other objects. Neither does he react in a purely physical way to physical in-fringements upon his organism. There is a nonphysical or trans-physical level to man's being. He is not just a reactor but an inquirer. Man is conscious, and his consciousness, unlike that of any other animal, is reflective so that he knows both self and other. Moreover, he knows that he knows. His consciousness is rational, which among other things means that it is a question-ing consciousness. No answer received or worked out is ever final. Man can always ask another question.

Reality for this questioning being is never just physical or material. Because of the peculiar form of man's consciousness, reality emerges for the human person as symbol, i.e., as physical but also as something more. Every object for man bears mean-ing. The horse, the dog, and the man may be in the same place, but only for man does the surrounding physical reality emerge as symbol. Only for man is there a field which not only pro-duces grain but also symbolizes the fertility and the affluence of nature. On the horizon there is for man a mountain which di-vides one area from another but also symbolizes man's insignifi-cance and provides the seeds of contemplation. Running nearby is a stream from which all three might drink but only for man is it called a stream and only for him does its water symbolize purity, refreshment, and forgiveness. Of the three only man sits and reflects about himself and the world. Man can live beyond in the world of contemplation because for him and him alone the world points beyond itself.

The meanings with which reality is imbued for man are not

his own alone. They are held in common with others. He was introduced to them by learning the language of a culture and by being taught its common beliefs. Man shares the meanings he contacts in the world around him so that gradually there is built up a *world* of meanings and a shared culture. We call man spiritual because he lives in this world of meanings or symbols which go beyond the purely physical. He does more than just react physically to material objects. Because he lives at this other level man is a responder rather than a reactor. He is born into a world of shared interpretations in interaction with which he forms himself. This spiritual world does not dictate or determine him. Man chooses his own response to the meanings and interpretations which permeate his existence. Man is not like things in the world. He is not even the most marvelous of all the things. Things are physical. Man is spiritual. He is a no-thing.

Man lives by meanings as much as he does by bread. His spiritual life is as important as his physical existence. The fact that there is this spiritual dimension to human existence, however, does not mean that the physical is lower or of lesser importance. Man is a unity. There is disorder and fragmentation even in the realm of the spiritual. There is a gap between man's meanings (more or less adequate for him) and the adequacy or completeness man searches for. Man's spirituality as much as his physical being manifests lack, imperfection, and nonbeing. No matter how solid or sound the meanings, the human being can always ask a further question. Science is a testimony to the continuing questioning that goes on between man and his world. Not even a scientific explanation is ever finished. Every scientific "fact" needs interpretation and is open to further inquiry. No matter how sacred the meaning it always suggests a further question. Only death will quiet man's reflective, questioning consciousness.

Meaning plays an important role in every aspect of man's life. Shared meanings make human community. Independently of their adequacy or truth value, meanings form human groups and are held on to by members of a group with surprising vigor. Wars are fought, with all their cruelty and loss of life, whenever shared systems of meaning come into conflict. Men fight for symbols and not just for economic causes as Marx proposed. The reason is understandable: man needs human community. Man lives with his fellows. The human group, however, is possible only where there are shared interpretations. Threats to shared symbols are threats to life.

Meanings or symbols do not just float around in disarray within man's mind. Each person puts meanings together into patterns of belief. Man's belief system in turn organizes the world for him. Coherence is created and chaos avoided by the ordering of meanings into an overall pattern which we call a belief system or a philosophy. By putting his meanings together in a certain way man tries to make sense out of his existence. He not only experiences reality as symbol but experiences as well the need for order and unity in his symbols. Meaningfulness requires coherence and consistency. If the patterns according to which this coherence is attained come under attack or even are ridiculed, man himself is threatened. In the same way a whole society can fall apart when it loses faith in its basic meanings. Even confusion in a belief system causes grave turmoil. A man is not like a rock which is a finished reality, out there in its place fully and completely. Man can and does come unstuck. Keeping oneself together is a good that is vulnerable both to physical attacks and also to attacks on a meaning system or his spiritual life. Spiritual death in the sense of loss of basic meanings is for some more terrible and more feared than physical death.

Where man's belief system is strong so that he can participate in his meanings, man experiences well-being. Man is full of life to the extent that he is able to participate in meanings, be they originally his own or those of others. When a man lives in his meanings, he is strong. Isolation from meaning-giving reality is a slow and a sad death. When life ceases to make sense man ceases to live it. Look at the scientist or the poet who lives in his meanings. His work is not work. His life is filled with energy, interest, and excitement. The intense participation in a world of meanings not only creates new meanings but it also creates the human self. Man affirms himself spiritually by discovering meanings or participating in them. He cannot live just by amassing things and gaining power. "Not by bread alone . . ."

The collapse of meaning is one of the major causes of emotional illness today. Victor Frankl has developed a psychotherapeutic technique called logotherapy in which the efforts of the therapist are directed toward the establishment of a meaning system for and with the patient. Frankl saw the high incidence of severe mental disorder caused today by the absence of substantial meaning in interaction with which a person might make his life. Our age for Frankl is characterized by a breakdown in the traditional meaning systems and this in turn has had a disastrous effect upon man's life. The central factor in human existence is seen as the will to meaning. Any loss of meaning causes a corresponding loss of humanness. Only by recovering a sound meaning system can contemporary man recover his mental balance. Many years ago Nietzsche insisted that European man needed meanings to live and die by. Frankl is just one more voice attesting to the spiritual dimension of human existence. Without something to believe in man's spiritual life collapses. Unless help is received, physical death is usually not far behind.

Doubt, Meaninglessness, Courage

The threats to man's spiritual life are legion. The belief system which organizes reality for man is built upon some fundamental meaning, one that holds together all the others. This basic meaning is not a rock. It can be and oftentimes is dissolved. Threats to meanings, including fundamental meanings, come from within man himself as well as from the outside. Either inner doubts, or changes in the objective reality which meanings organize, can pull down a particular meaning or even the most basic one on which all the others rest. The proliferation of proposed new meaning systems from black Muslimism to devil worship to yoga and astrology testifies to the fact that for many people the more traditional fundamental meanings have disintegrated. People today rush from one coven, to another sect, to another temple, and the meaning of each seems to vanish as quickly as the enthusiasm for it developed in the first place. The passion reflected in the search shows the importance of a meaning system for man's life. In fact, not only is physical death preferred to loss of a meaning-giving system, but suicide very frequently follows a loss of faith. There is, for example, a high rate of suicide among the returned prisoners of war who after years of confinement and brainwashing have nothing left to believe in. The fact that psychiatrists have the highest suicide rate in America might be related to the absence of concern on the part of Freud with man's spirituality.

For a time it is possible for man to force belief, but an adequate belief system cannot be just the result of strong desire. Meaning has to be adequate in and by itself. Meanings have to be able to withstand the functioning of man's critical consciousness and the enduring pressure of its questions. They also have to stand the pressure of external events. They have to make sense of external reality. Reality speaks back to man in terms of experience and every meaning system must be able to handle this dialogue. No system can be maintained in the face of an alien reality. Or better, a system can be maintained in the face of an alien reality only at the price of sanity.

Man's spiritual life is just as real and just as universal as his physical life. The only way to abdicate from the pressures of spirituality is to abdicate from life. The fact is that man has this spiritual side and the only remaining question is how well he handles the threats to which it is exposed. As in the case of man's physical reality there are healthy and unhealthy types of response. Courage again will be the key to a healthy response and psychic fulfillment. Escape from his situation will in every case produce sickness. Courage in this context means spiritual self-affirmation, the affirming of oneself in the face of threat to one's meanings.

Questioning which takes the form of doubting is, as we have seen, one of the unique dimensions of man's consciousness. There is nothing wrong with having doubts. Rather, there is everything wrong with not having them. Doubting is both a creative and a potentially destructive function of man's mind. Man participates in his meanings but never does he so identify with them that doubts disappear. There is always a gap between man and his belief system which permits its being questioned and doubted. Spirituality involves doubting and yet doubting can grow until it absorbs all meaning and destroys spirituality. Doubt, just as effectively as changing events, can pull down the meaning system in which man lives. Even the poet and the scientist have doubts about their involvement with a particular world of meaning. Doubts are not confined to the world of religious belief. Human life is full of doubts. To be a human being is to live exposed to the risks which doubt engenders.

A failure of courage leads to unhealthy and ultimately dehumanizing ways of handling doubt. An example of this is the suppression of all doubting—a phenomenon we call fanaticism. Rather than facing up to the human condition, and to the threats to meaning that inevitably are generated by questioning, the fanatic suppresses questioning altogether. He guarantees the stability of his meaning system by refusing to permit any questioning or doubts about it. He is afraid of losing a meaning system and the hell of meaninglessness. Rather than suffer this peculiar form of emptiness he imposes meanings upon himself authoritatively. He insists that they be so imposed on others as well. In order to avoid the anxiety associated with threats to meaning, the fanatic gives up the human form of consciousness altogether. In order to avoid the risk of questioning he gives up questioning. He manages to save his meanings but he does so at the expense of his human being.

Hearst is an example of unhealthy response to man's physical dimension. He tried to reduce or diminish a part of himself and tried to suppress part of the outside world as well. The same type of thing happens with the fanatic believer or the fanatic unbeliever. Each represses the questioning self and tries to repress part of the world as well, lest questioning upset his narrow existence. Paradoxically, however, as in the case of Hearst, rather than escaping from the threat, one's whole life winds up being dominated by it. The fanatic is weak. He is afraid of questions. He cannot affirm himself or keep himself together in the face of questions and this weakness ultimately does him in.

What better solutions are open to the human person? We

come back again to the same requirement for being truly human —courage. Since man's life involves an interaction with meanings and since these are open to incessant questioning because of the very structure of the human mind, the only realistic response is the courage to affirm one's self, in the midst of constant inquiry and doubt. Doubting and questioning have a positive and a negative side. Potentially they are destructive, but man must have the courage to promote them despite this threat. On the positive side, one of man's glories is his questioning and inquiring. Admittedly it is difficult, but a person can hold to a meaning system, participate in the meanings, believe, and yet remain always open to inquiry, other meanings, and different points of view. Openness and willingness to reexamine even the most fundamental meanings are the tests of healthy people. Such an attitude is not to be confused with creeping disbelief or suspicion or a wishy-washy attitude. Firm commitment to meaning and values is compatible with a constantly inquiring consciousness, given the presence of courage.

Because of his inquisitiveness man, like God, can become creative and make new what never was. Healthy self-affirmation does not try to escape from what man is, but rather embraces human life and lives it. The necessary courage is more easily spoken than practiced but man's whole life depends upon it. Courage is needed in the face of death and sickness and limitation. No less courage is needed in the face of spiritual death, emptiness, and meaninglessness.

Chapter 6

Man as Ethical Despite Himself

The same scientific approach which excluded man's spirituality from consideration also eliminated the ethical dimension of human existence. Freud attended to man's physical drives and assumed that these operated deterministically. Physical science presupposes that the material world is understandable by measurement and that its movements are ruled by laws. That very same supposition was applied to the human being by those who insisted that science is the only way of knowing. Freud, for example, changed his mind on certain issues throughout his development but never abandoned the idea of himself as a scientist and never recognized the limitations of this methodology. Freedom in such an approach has to be an illusion because man's behavior like that of other physical elements in the universe is ruled by law. Every effect (act, or behavior) is assumed to have a cause which determines it, so that once science isolates or identifies the causes it can with complete reliability predict what man will do.

Freud the scientist denied freedom, calling it an illusion, and yet later, in discussing psychoanalysis, he reintroduced freedom as the very goal of therapy. The mentally ill patient acts compulsively, i.e., in a determined way, and successful therapy must bring such a person to the point of controlling his or her behavior. Freud consistently uses self-control as a standard for a

61

mature or healthy person and the absence of such as a sure characteristic of illness. Psychoanalysis as therapy aims at extending the patient's control and correspondingly responsibility for his actions. Freud's scientistic presuppositions led him to deny the existence of freedom but his common sense and his experience with life led him to reintroduce the term, which obviously refers to an aspect of every human life. Those "even more scientific" students of the human (the followers of Skinner) have their theoretical blinders even more firmly fixed and are more dedicated to logical consistency than was Freud. Despite the everyday evidence to the contrary, they continue to insist that freedom is impossible. Skinner himself went so far as to say at the end of one of his articles that he could claim no responsibility or praise for what he had done because it was all determined. Anyone who has ever written for publication will marvel at the extent to which Skinner's philosophical faith overcomes the most forceful and obvious experience. No article writes itself and the writer knows how much *will* is required, how much personal initiative is involved, and the degree to which each writer is responsible for what he says. Choice, initiative, control, recognition of alternatives, decision, and finally responsibility—all these make up the package of experience which can be referred to as ethical.

Freedom and Choice

Man is not exhausted in his physical and spiritual dimensions. Besides a given physical reality with its built-in limitations and the spiritual reality with its constant struggle for coherence, man is by nature also an ethical being. Ethics is not some ideal set of norms to which man may or may not give assent. It is as much a part of being human as space and time and meanings. Man is condemned to be ethical because choice cannot be escaped any more than death or doubt.

In the animal kingdom we find a set of biological capacities related to sets of outside stimuli. Given both poles, a reaction or a set of reactions is possible. There is a dynamic equilibrium between the animal's biology and the situation in which it finds itself. The adjustment of the animal to its surroundings is determined by its biological capacities. To some degree man shares the animal condition. Man's organism (especially his brain), however, is considerably more complex than that of the animal. Because of this no one reaction is adequate to his situation. The condition to which man responds is itself enormously complex and greatly increases the number of options open to him. The complexity, both internal and external, makes impossible any single reaction. As a result the human animal finds himself suspended before his situation without a determined or automatic reaction. The freedom of man in the first and most basic sense means to be free from the configurations of stimuli with which he is bombarded. He can shut them out or he can permit them to operate. He can react or not react. He can react one way or another. In order to survive, given this situation, man must take cognizance of the situation, assess it, and consider alternatives. He must perform all the functions which we associate with intelligence. For the human animal the outside becomes an environment rather than a set of stimuli, and his surroundings become a world.

Man's freedom is associated both with his unique symbolic consciousness and with his intelligence. Both these spiritual capacities are in turn founded on his complex physical organism. The physical, the spiritual, and the ethical are all part of what we call human nature or the structure of human existence. One cannot speak of human freedom as if it were purely spiritual and in no way dependent upon man's biology. The French philosopher Sartre is unsuccessful in his attempt to found freedom on nothing. Not only is it related to man's peculiar biology but it is also inseparable from his peculiar intelligence. True freedom cannot be irrational. Freedom disassociated from mind is destructive and degenerates quickly into unfreedom. We can discover evidently distinguishable dimensions of human existence, but they all go together to make man, a unitary being.

To say that man is free does not mean that he is perfectly free or that his freedom is without limits. There are certain instinctual or quasi-instinctual reactions generated by the contact between man's complex biological apparatus and the outside world. After all, man developed from the animal kingdom and retains many similarities with his unreflecting brothers. Obviously missing in man, however, is the natural adjustment between the animal and his surroundings. All of man's responses are not built into the connection between himself and this world. Given the separation between man and his surroundings the human animal does not *adjust*. Man must *make just* his response or *just*ify his acts. He cannot escape this responsibility because it is founded on his physical and spiritual structures. Man's free actions have no built-in justice. Justice must be given to the human responses by man himself. Man makes justice. Man is condemned by his freedom to build justice into his acts because there is no automatic ad*just*ment. He may define justice in many ways and construct greatly diverse standards of behavior, but he cannot escape responsibility for the character of his acts. Man is condemned to be ethical.

Nonbeing threatens man in his ethical dimension just as much as it does in the physical and the spiritual. Absence, lack, deficiency infect man's free decisions just as they do the physical and spiritual levels of his being. Man's freely chosen behavior, his initiations toward others, the responses he makes to the situations in which he finds himself, are all shot through with nonbeing. It is not enough to say that these are never perfect. In many cases the deficiency is directly attributable to what man could have done and did not, or to a distortion for which he is directly responsible. The justice he is required to build into his acts is absent so that it is also correct to say that man is condemned to be unethical.

The freely chosen actions which man himself must construct and for which he must bear responsibility are not confined to actions in or on the world. Man must justify or make *himself* just, as well as the outside world in which he operates. Even though his physical and spiritual dimensions are given and not a result of his choosing, man's response to these is not given and *is* the result of his choice. Man's freedom is not just a freedom from external stimuli, but a positive freedom to construct one or another way of responding to everything, including his own life.

Man's physical and spiritual dimensions are both given to man and also demanded of him, in the sense that he is required by his freedom to answer for himself, to make decisions about himself, to make his own life and make it just. Man is an ethical animal in the most severe sense; i.e., he must choose even his own life. His freedom means that even his responses to himself are of his own choosing. By his choices, by the exercise of his freedom, by his ethical behavior, man makes his life.

If man's actions, his behavior, indeed his very being are both given to him and demanded of him, then man is free and at the same time faces a threat from the nonbeing or defects of his freedom. What is demanded of him (the making of his own life by his free choices) is also judged by him and by others. Because man is structurally ethical he stands of necessity under the cloak of justice and judgment. If he must choose his responses even to his life, then he must suffer the anxiety which precedes such decisions. He must just as surely suffer the guilt that follows the choice which is deficient or distorted. The lack of justice in his choices and the self created by these are man's own doing.

The realization that my life is to some extent what I choose to make it is an awesome one. The realization that my behavior and my very life are what I choose to make them causes anxiety. We sense this anxiety most strongly at crossroads. When we have to choose and know that our life will be very different according as we move in one or another direction, anxiety presses in on us. Unless we have destroyed our moral sensitivities we feel a lesser anxiety in the many daily situations that call for a response. Each response, each choice, stands under a judgment. Neither our actions nor our choices nor our life escapes the inevitable nonbeing that permeates the human reality. Even man's best efforts are imperfect; some of his choices and behavior are downright evil.

Because man's freedom like everything else about him is limited, there are many aspects of his behavior that are either fixed or at least somewhat independent of any choosing. His fixed reality (e.g., his face or his parents) is, however, fringed by possibility. He is not infinitely free but there is a freedom within limits that corresponds to the possibility that inhabits the most obviously determined aspects of his being. His parents are fixed but there are many possible responses he may make to them. The same is true with every part of man's life. Someone might consider his present situation to have been caused by circumstances beyond his control, but he is aware that there are still open to him a number of different possible responses or behaviors. Man is called upon to make his life within certain limits but nonetheless to make his life. Each life choice contributes to the creation of the self that is at the same time already there but not yet fully there or terminally constituted. Life choices actualize the possibilities which fringe man's self and his world.

Ethics as a part of philosophy occupies itself with this aspect of human being. It attempts to analyze the components of human acts, assess degrees of autonomy and responsibility, describe the image of perfection in human self-creation, etc. Ethics, among other things, develops norms for man to live by and standards according to which he should make his self-constituting choices. Ethics, however, is not exhausted by what goes by that name in philosophy. Each man has the power to go with or go against any norm, whether it comes from God or man. The most lowly man can choose to contradict any law, even the law he may have given himself. (Man like no other animal has the power to contradict himself.) Man can choose not to actualize the fringe of possibility that surrounds his being and thereby not fulfill his destiny. Only man can lose himself.

Anxiety, Guilt, Courage

Because man can fail totally in the life project and inevitably fails to some degree in it, he experiences guilt. Human consciousness accompanies man's wrong choices and this awareness we call guilt. Admittedly, a great deal of guilt is social in the sense that it originates in the judgments society makes on us. It is, however, not totally social. Because man's knowledge goes along with his actions and his choices, he has a conscience (*cum* plus *scire*, a *knowing* that goes *with*). Man by his reflective awareness stands over against himself and judges himself.

The atheism of Jean Paul Sartre, which flees from a God who judges, puts in his place a self-judgment which is cruel and unforgiving. Atheism is no escape from conscience, because conscience and judgment belong to the structure of man. Just as surely is guilt a part of man's condition because the judgment cannot always be positive. Being guilty, like facing death, or struggling for meaning, is part of the human condition. The fact that it is always present to some degree does not mean that it is always handled well. It can lead to very destructive types of self-rejection and despair. All sorts of neuroses and psychoses can come from guilt feelings. On the other hand, guilt can prod a person toward improvement and needed changes in life style. Everything depends upon the response.

There are sick and healthy responses to man's ethical dimension, his conscience and guilt. The sick responses are legion. Take, for example, moral anarchy. Rather than face guilt and its corresponding anxiety some choose to escape by denying the ethical structure of man and rejecting the existence of judgment on their acts. For the moral anarchist there are no standards, no laws, and no negative judgments. No one is guilty because there is no freedom and there are no norms. This position, also referred to as *anomism*, prefers to deny the structure of man to bearing the pain of guilt or judgment. This particular form of escape is common in radicals and revolutionists who, despite their displays of defiance, are actually weak personalities, so weak in fact that the very suggestion that they are responsible for their lives is unbearable. They prefer to blame society for their self-hatred. This in turn justifies destroying it.

Another unhealthy reaction to man's situation is moral rigor or what in Catholic moral tradition is referred to as *legalism*. When faced with the reality of self-judgment or guilt the legalists, like the anarchists, try to escape. Flight here, however, is not away from all law but toward a literal and unbending identification with law. To avoid judgment and the anxiety associated with guilt the legalist makes law the whole of life. Existence becomes confined to the parameters of the law. Unless covered by law no action is ventured. Where the law prohibits not even a possibility for action is entertained. Life for the anarchist is chaotic. For the legalist it is rigid and dry. In both cases paradoxically the guilt and anxiety which were unbearable remain and indeed are increased. The legalist literally becomes eaten up with anxiety over compliance with the law. He worries himself to death about every minute detail of every action and every law. The anxiety of the anarchist is not quite so close to the surface but it is just as surely present and tends to break out under stress in the form of despair. On the surface the despair is about society. In fact it is always a despair about the self.

Although anxiety about death and meanings is different from that about life choices, the three forms are interconnected. An anxiety over death can be increased by a consciousness of guilt. By the same token the moral anarchist who anxiously flees from guilt tends also to have an unhealthy attitude toward death. In some cases, the fear of death becomes a fascination and life becomes a series of anarchistic actions expressing a death wish. In other cases, the selfsame moral anarchist becomes obsessed by the fear of death or any form of suffering and in unguarded moments shows himself to be a coward. (In his play, *No Exit*, Sartre shows the radical journalist to be in fact a weakling and a coward.) Giving in to the pain of moral anxiety can also be associated with a collapse of meanings. Meaninglessness can cause a loss of moral nerve. Doubts and skepticism can undermine established moral standards or even the very existence of man's ethical dimension.

In this ethical area as in the other two, the key to a healthy response is courage. Conscience is a reality. So is self-judgment. Anxiety and guilt are inevitable dimensions of man. In order that these may not overwhelm man he must stand up to them. To be a man is to affirm oneself in the face of anxiety and guilt. Rather than trying by legalism or anarchism to escape the situation, man needs courage. Strength is required to face this aspect of his nonbeing. Guilt and anxiety point to the need for man to do better. They point to man's condition as unfinished, surrounded by ambiguity and nevertheless called to something more. Anxiety and guilt then are pointers to what man must struggle for. In order that they may play this role, however, man must have the courage to go on making himself, choosing, taking responsibility, aspiring after a justice in his life, and all this despite the failures, the ambiguities, the anxiety, and the guilt.

To say that man's guilt is structural or existential means that it belongs to the very constitution of human existence. It does not mean that man must go around beating his breast. Nor does it mean that he must take flight into some fictitious existence. Man is going to be guilty and guilt should not be ignored. It should be read as a symbol of something better to which man is called. At the same time man must affirm himself in the face of guilt. The self can be affirmed in spite of guilt. Self-affirmation is the courage to go on, despite guilt, despite the threat of death, despite the elements of doubt in the meanings by which we live. The alternatives to courage are various forms of neurotic and psychotic behavior. Despair is the opposite of self-affirmation and the other pole of courage.

There is a physical dimension of man and therefore he faces suffering and death. Man's spiritual dimension means that he must face meaninglessness and doubt. The inevitable ethical level of human life throws man against guilt and judgment. The anxiety associated with each aspect of life can overcome man and throw him into despair. Life then is a struggle against despair. Not that every day man trembles on this ominous abyss, but every life must walk along the abyss from time to time and sense its danger. It is in light of the insight provided by those special times that we gain a privileged view into the human situation. Facing death means that life is understood differently. The same is so with regard to meaninglessness and guilt. We should not assume that each day brings a confrontation with a collapse of meaning or a serious sense of moral deficiency, but when these do arise, they show up an all-important aspect of the human being. The limit situations of man (death, meaninglessness, guilt) are pointers to an understanding of the structure of human existence.

Chapter 7

Man, the Lover

When we talk about freedom and meanings, and a consciousness of space and time, as constituents of human being, we are obviously thinking about adult human existence. For the adult there is a certain gap or separation from the reality which surrounds him. Because of this gap the human person is required to construct his responses, and such construction in turn requires intelligence. The gap makes the world emerge over and against man so that he can grasp its structure. The human being perceives the outside not as raw data but rather as symbol and meaning which to some extent he constructs and is responsible for. All this, however, points to a prior problem. What is the nature of the reality out of which freedom and meaning develop? From whence do thought and choice set out? The very existence of meanings and freedom is a product of a later development in man, but a development from what? What is man's original world—the one which preceded the division of reality into subject and object?

Relationship and Oneness

The answer is suggested by the formulation of the question. Before division there was unity. Before the gap there was a oneness. Initially, the human self and the world are one. For the baby, there is no gap or division but one simple reality. Frontiers or boundaries where the self stops and the world begins come later. With the learning of language, a break appears between child and world. Before language, however, the human being is a lived participation, a unity, a oneness with others and the world. This starting point is all-important because it indicates the direction which man's fulfillment will take. The question of human beginning—that state out of which thought and freedom develop—both marks the point of departure and suggests the goal toward which man will tend in his development. Becoming fully human means to strive for a recovery of an original oneness. Man is a physical being who faces death, a spiritual being who struggles for depth and coherence in meanings, an ethical being who is condemned to construct his own responses to surrounding reality, and finally, man is a drive toward the other—a drive to overcome the separation of himself from both the world and other people. In effect, man is a social being.

When in philosophy there is talk about sociality it means more than that human beings like to get together for parties. The fact that human life begins in participation and only in later development becomes separate points to a much more radical sociality. Because the human being begins life in a oneness with all, a recovery of this oneness is the built-in goal of man's being. Just as surely as meanings and freedom are associated with the gap which separates man and his world, sociality in the sense of various forms of unity is a natural human goal. Love, friendship, fidelity are just as much a part of the human condition as intelligence, imagination, and freedom. Human life, besides its physical, spiritual, and ethical dimensions, is social. Fulfillment as it relates to this social dimension involves a recovery of the original oneness in which life begins. To be human means to be called to relationship. Human being is a drive toward unity with the other, understood not only as the individualized other person but also the generalized other: nature, the group, the culture, the society. Man's sociality is both essential and a many-splendored thing.

Human love is just one manifestation of man's social being. Love is as much a part of human life as meanings, freedom, or death. Man becomes himself in deep intimate relationships.

Love and other manifestations of his radical sociality belong to man as man. The oneness with the world and other people which full humanness requires is not the "dumb" or unreflecting unity with which life begins but rather a unity that does not ignore the developments in man of freedom and intelligence. The original preconceptual or instinctual unity points to another oneness to be recovered which involves all the other dimensions of mature human existence. Human love is the recovery of an original oneness and is never separate from either intelligence or freedom.

Besides being a lover, man is also a politician. His drive toward unity with the other includes the generalized other—what we call culture or society. On the interpersonal level man gestures in speech and action toward his fellows and strives to bring about a harmony between himself and the other. (Man presses for an ever richer unification—toward a perfect at-*one*-ment.) The same is so on the less personal level of man's relationship with his group and his culture. Life begins in a kind of oneness here also. Man worries about the quality of his relationship with his culture and its institutions just as he does about his interpersonal life. His intentionality stretches him toward both the other individual and the generalized patterns of his culture. This aspect of his being makes man a political animal. A denial of politics then in the sense of a withdrawal of man from interaction with his cultural environment is a denial of an aspect of man's being.

Since man's original oneness includes the physical world as well as the social world and other individuals, man's drive toward recovery of the original oneness includes also a new relatedness with physical reality. The development in man of reflective consciousness splits the original oneness into a subject-object dichotomy, but such is not the end of man's development. Because man the subject is separate he can understand, use, control, analyze the object. But because life began in a unity and points toward reunion, to remain exclusively in the mode of subject-object separation amounts to retarded or truncated development. The very possibility of another form of relationship with the world has recently been rediscovered in the youth culture and is being reintroduced into contemporary culture. The revival of meditation, both Eastern and Western styles, is making possible a unitive consciousness even with the physical world. The mountain, the tree, the plain become not just something over against me, but part of myself. Meditation puts man into a new relationship, a unitive relationship with physical being from which life developed and with which it retains an intimate relationship.

The breakup of the original unity of man with reality might be called an alienation, but an altogether necessary one. This breakup, associated with the development of language, is accompanied by an awareness in the self of its separateness. Children who begin to speak begin to experience themselves as separate. Closely associated with learning the words for daddy and mommy and chair is the awareness of an I, and the beginning of references to me, me, me. Some thinkers understand the Adam and Eve story as symbolic of the fall of man out of a oneness with nature, characteristic of the animal kingdom, into the separateness of human existence, which in turn is always associated with some form of guilt and shame. Man's break with nature, then, is a two-sided coin. It is the beginning of man's superiority and an alienation which causes guilt and shame.

The loss of the paradisiacal oneness is the precondition for the possibility of thought and freedom, and is also the foundation of man's drive for relationship. Man first must break the harmony of the prehuman state and then begin a lifelong pursuit of new unities and harmonies with both other persons and the natural and social world. Man, then, is a paradox. In one respect his fall from the original harmony, accompanied by anxiety, guilt, and shame, makes man a sick animal. Separation from nature is a disruption or a disorder. On the other hand, separation is the condition for the possibility of intelligence, freedom, and finally the higher forms of unity and harmony which we refer to as friendship, love, concern, respect, fidelity. Once man leaves the original world (the result of an original sin?) there is no way for him to return. (The gates of the garden are locked.) The only possibility which remains is to strive for new harmonies, both with the world and with his fellows. Any attempt to return to the original or prehuman oneness becomes a regression and leads to a diminution of humanness (psychosis or neurosis). Once born, man cannot go back to the womb.

Man's separateness is first of all a consciousness of his separation, a new form of intelligence we call self-awareness. Man knows he is the subject of his experiences and knows that in this he is alone. There is no interchangeability of experience. The oridinary experience of mature man separates him from all that he is not. This experience which lifts man out of nature is intimately associated, as we have already mentioned, with language. The new separate existence does not come all at once. Only gradually does man develop conceptual categories which in turn refine and deepen his experience of himself as set over and against his environment. The birth of man from the animal as well as the birth of each individual human being is an evolutionary process.

Only because the self is separate from the world and from others can it learn to think about and use what it finds at hand. Science is a natural development of man's capacity to view reality from a distance. Human survival in the world involves a moving away from things in order to gain mastery over them. Man's possibilities for control of things is almost without limit. Man can, however, become so engrossed in the domination of things necessary for survival that he becomes bogged down in that particular type of relationship. As necessary and beneficial as science and technology are for man, they constitute a temptation to rest and remain in that mode. Man can become so occupied with use, manipulation, measuring, analyzing, describing, and cataloguing all that stands over and against him that he neglects the effort to move toward the reconquest of that oneness with which his life began. Man in a culture dominated by science and technology has shown a marked tendency toward mechanical relationships instead of love, concern, responsibility for another. The possibilities opened up by man's split with reality tend to overshadow and even hide another set of possibilities for oneness and relationship which are so intimately tied to man's fulfillment.

Distorted Love, Authentic Love, Courage

It has been said of contemporary man that he has gained control over the whole world and suffered the loss of his soul. He has not attended to the promotion of all the dimensions of his sociality and consequently his technical, scientific advances tend to threaten his human relationships and ultimately his very species. Man's development has been lopsided. His advance in one direction (domination of the natural other) has not been accompanied by an advance in another just as necessary direction (unity with the natural other and the personal other). Because he has not attended to this aspect of sociality, he stands in danger of crushing that very human spirit which springs only from unitive human relationships. Man cannot survive without development of possibilities rising out of the subject/object split. He cannot survive either without development of the possibilities for overcoming the split through various forms of harmony and unity.

Unless man's evolution is more than scientific or technological, the enormous project of contemporary civilization will be a lost effort. Unless man also develops in the direction of love, he will end up a monster. The other person is not a thing. Rather, the other human persons set limits to man's capacity for control. A self-awareness and separation that generates only power over the other ultimately leads to the destruction of both the other and the self. If man tries to reduce his fellowman to a manageable object or a tool he literally destroys both his fellowman and himself. The master is as much a victim of domination as the slave. Separation founds the drive to reunite and this must be kept alive in the face of threats from a drive to control and dominate. A man can repress and even conceivably destroy within himself this quest for unity and harmony with the other and by so doing he destroys his own being. Not only does man's sanity depend upon his development of the capacity for that peculiar form of harmony we call love, but his very being depends on it. Man's quest for love is a quest for humanness. It is the drive which stands behind the whole gamut of human passions. The many contemporary forms of violence and destruction are only twisted or disordered forms of relationship.

Nowhere is the threat of nonbeing more obvious or more ominous than in the area of man's sociality. The threats to love, for instance, are like so many demons warring against man's fulfillment. The classic forms of twisted or disordered love are masochism and sadism. Love becomes twisted either into submission or into domination. The masochist overcomes separateness along with the corresponding feelings of isolation and insecurity by attaching himself like a parasite to another who protects him. It is a form of unity, but a deficient one. The other is inflated beyond reasonable limits. The self is deflated into an appendage. Unity here is achieved at the expense of one's own independence. Individual freedom and consciousness are sacrificed to the drive for reunion. The self is not fulfilled, but diminished. Masochism is unity without integrity.

Sadism is the same disorder in the opposite form. In masochism, passivity is the characteristic of love's disorder. In sadism, it is activity or domination which is the sign of disease. Separation, isolation, fear, and insecurity are overcome by reducing the other to a part of oneself. The sadist commands, exploits, even physically hurts the other while the masochist submits to these forms of behavior. Like masochism, sadism is a form of unity but not a healthy one. In both cases, one or the other self is turned into a thing. Since the drive in human beings is toward fulfillment with another self, this is frustrated as long as one of the participants is a thing or a nonperson. Because both are distorted forms of one and the same human need, sadism and masochism often are found together. The sadist in one set of circumstances becomes the masochist in another, and vice versa. In either case, human love is distorted, and fulfillment is eluded.

Authentic love differs from both in that it is a unity which does not destroy either the self or the other. It is a harmony with integrity. It is a unity shot through with justice. This unity heals the scars of the original separation and leads man to heights of being, unknown in the animal kingdom. It is an approach to the other which listens and is patient. It is a giving of the self that saves the self. It is an act of generosity which paradoxically makes the giver richer and stronger. In love man experiences himself as full to overflowing. Love then is the recovery of an original unity but on a higher level, one which does not ignore but rather perfects the many other aspects of man's being. Love makes the human spirit. It includes giving, caring, listening, forgiving, responsibility, and respect. It is the perfection of man's sociality.

Through consciousness and language, man becomes separate. Through love he is reunited in a higher form with the personal elements in his primordial unity. Love and consciousness then go together. Not only are they complementary, they are also interwoven. Reflective consciousness makes the reunion of love possible and necessary. Love in turn is another way of perfecting understanding and awareness. Especially with regard to the other human being, love is the only way of really knowing the other. Human beings are never known from the outside, no matter how sophisticated the equipment with which they are approached. Only the experience of union gives deep and adequate understanding of the other person. The act of union is fulfilling for man, even with respect to his powers of understanding. Love leads to an understanding of both the self and the other. I can know neither myself nor the other from the outside or objectively. In loving the other, I penetrate the other's secret. In so doing, I also penetrate the secret of my own being. In love man finds himself, enlightens himself, and discovers what it is to be human.

Besides the many tendencies within man himself to twist love into something it is not, there are enormous pressures coming from contemporary society against this particular form of man's social fulfillment. Despite the obvious benefits of deep loving relationships for human beings, very little is done in today's society to stimulate, promote, and support such behavior. In fact, society seems to push man in the very opposite direction. The diabolically contrived disruptions of human relationships in the Nazi concentration camps seem to be exaggerated instances of the sickness pervading the whole of contemporary culture. Trust and openness, the preconditions for love's development, are systematically undermined. It takes substantial amounts of suspicion and subterfuge to get along in today's world. Concern for the other, self-sacrifice for another, even in their most rudimentary forms are every day more difficult in a culture which forms people in patterns of selfishness. In our consumer society, getting things, saving things, eating and drinking things—these are held up as signs of happiness and fulfillment. Fear of the other rather than any form of love is the more usual mode of relationships. The other becomes a competitor in the pursuit of things. Society seems gradually to be pushing man to become again a "wolf" to his fellowman (*homo homini lupus*). Our culture celebrates violence and destruction and does so to such an extent that these become accepted, though obviously diseased, forms of human relationships.

Explaining our sad situation is much easier than turning the situation around. The culturally institutionalized hatred of other races is deeply embedded in the American way and its seeds never cease to bear fruit. Inequities in economics always breed disrespect and disorder in relationships. The most fundamental problem, however, remains the idolatry of things. Man becomes wedded to machines or even worse an appendage to them in order to produce commodities. This lowers him and diminishes his capacity for loving. He is further diminished by being turned into a consumer or a customer whose value is only as great as his capacity to buy. Man as consumer is manipulated and enslaved by subtle forms of propaganda which not only diminish him as a person but in the process distort the fundamental values of truth and love. Truth is subverted by advertisement and love is turned into the by-product of some hair spray or underarm deodorant. The dehumanization is furthered by classifying man in certain economic categories and filing them in a computer which does not take into account his creative qualities or his uniquely human capacities. How can man so divested of human substance develop respect for his being? The idolatry of things tends to make man a thing and thereby gradually destroy his capacity for love and truly human being. Death is much with us in all its horrible forms because the value of human life and life-fulfilling activities has been bargained away for a houseful of junk.

The decline of love and all that promotes loving relationships is both reflected in the dominant images of man and caused by these images. Man lives by the image he has of himself, and the great contemporary image makers are literally the makers of modern man. Again it is science that dictates the type of image created. Freud, for example, found in man what his methodology permitted him to find: physical drives, urges, instincts. Concentrating on the cellar of human existence he found the most powerful form of the drive toward the other, sex. Man for Freud was a sexual being but not a lover. In his *General Introduction to Psychoanalysis* (1915–16), one finds in the index innumerable references to sex but not a single reference to love. Just as the narrow methodology of the scientific approach limited Freud's perception of the role of freedom and meaning, it also obscured the importance of love and relationship. Freud saw man fulfilled in sexuality but missed the role of relationship in human life. Contemporary man is to a great extent Freudian man, made in the image of Freudian theory. As such he lacks *will* in the sense of self-choice (ethics) and a sense of the importance of deep loving relationship (sociality). Both these deficiencies promote his dehumanization.

Is there any way contemporary man can avoid the pressures of dehumanization and develop more fully his human being? Is it possible to resist the temptation to suppress the pain and anxiety associated with his present condition by immersing himself in the thousand petty tasks? How easy it is to become the slave to a schedule, a tireless worker (at home with a hobby when not at the plant), a student of stocks, etc., becoming all the time more intertwined with things. Turning life around so as to concentrate on all the dimensions of being human requires a conversion which is as radical as any reported in religious literature. Contemporary man needs a change of heart. He has to turn away from *doing*, toward *being*. "What does it profit a man to gain the whole world and suffer the loss of his soul?"

Becoming human is not automatic. It requires constant attention. Becoming an *ego* or an *individual* follows automatically the normal process of growth. Becoming a *person* (or a human self), however, is not automatic. In fact, it can be missed. Sören Kierkegaard tells the story of a man who lived his whole life and died, only then to discover that he had not really lived. Kierkegaard meant, of course, that he never gave sufficient attention or time to the development of human qualities. He had missed becoming a person. Kierkegaard's character stands for contemporary man who habitually gives no attention to his *being*. Courage is needed to change one's style of participating in life.

Love is a self-giving and who is there who is not overcome with anxiety in the face of such an act? If man chooses not to give himself, but to save his life, he loses it. Egoism is a failure of both courage and humanness. The egoist condemns himself to a self-constructed prison. Egoism is a move away from what leads to man's fulfillment, but overcoming egoism requires unusual strength and enduring courage. Because self-giving is such a difficult act (which paradoxically constitutes the self), many substitutes and facsimiles are resorted to. The most common of these is a contract for mutual sexual satisfaction, an egoism *à deux*. The popularity of that alternative can be judged by the extraordinary popularity of "how to do it" sex manuals. If mutual satisfaction is the basis of a relationship, then technique has a top priority. One might notice in contrast the absence of love manuals. The courage required for love makes it an uncommon gift.

Love is an opening of oneself to the other with all the anxiety associated with such a revelation. It is always easier to communicate on a more superficial level. It is far easier to put on a mask, to do what "is done" and say what "is said." Man puts on many different masks trying to avoid the more threatening revelations of his inner self. Love, however, is a communication from the center of one's being rather than a communication through appearances. It does not make use of the techniques for hiding one's center or real personality. As such it opens the real self to the possibility of rejection. To be rejected in one of our fronts or masks means that our inner self is still somewhat safe.

Rejection in the core of our being, however, is a form of death. Love, then, is a risk—the worst of all forms of risk, in fact, because the possibilities of failure involve a failure of one's whole self. Courage alone prepares a person for such a risk. Without courage man is condemned to a life of fronts and masks or, even worse, a life of abject isolation.

Love is forgiving, and courage is required to overcome the anxiety associated with that infrequent action. Why, one might ask, is forgiveness so much a part of love? The answer must be sought in power, which is a reality in every human encounter. It is so whether the encounter is friendly or hostile. Both persons are centers of power and inevitably human meeting is a kind of struggle. The power of each is to some extent a threat to the other. It is not unusual that there be conflict in love. Indeed, it is inevitable. Ideally, the power struggle should follow the rules of justice. Each person should be respected despite a degree of conflict. Domination or the threat of such should never be the goal of conflict. After all, the other is a person and not a dog or a brick. Injustice follows from ignoring this basic truth. Whenever domination occurs, or its lesser forms of compulsion, there is a degree of injustice. The injustice comes from the repression of the self which must be active and initiating. Abusive power destroys the power of the other to initiate.

Because such abuse is very common, even where there is a basic good will, there is frequent need for forgiveness. A popular slogan which comes out of the novel *Love Story* goes, "Love means you never have to say you're sorry." The very opposite is true. Love means you're always saying, "I'm sorry," and meaning it. Forgiveness does not hinge on the other's changing, reforming, or eliminating all reason for disagreement, but rather on his or her being accepted despite the enduring differences. Guilt follows upon injustice, and forgiveness is the way of overcoming both estrangement and guilt. There is no courage equal to that required to ask for forgiveness, or to forgive from the heart. The failure of this form of courage is the greatest single cause of love's failure.

In our "thingified" culture, personal existence has lost significance. Man's life becomes an instrument for goals outside himself. As early as high school, young people make lives subservient to a car or a motor bike. By college time, lives have oftentimes become means used and misused in order to gain things. Gradually human life itself turns into a thing. When man is alienated from the authentically human, a sense of loss and unfulfillment follows. In many cases man gradually comes to despise himself. Things, the pursuit of things, the care of things, should ideally be one of the garments which adorn the human animal but a garment which is light and does not burden man or restrict his movement. No one doubts that today things hang on us like iron bars. We carry our prison around with us.

The dangers to man posed by our culture, especially to man as a capacity and a need for deep relationships, are many and subtle. Things distract the human person from the fact that he is a no-thing. Deep concern, care, respect, responsibility, the giving of self to another, these are not thinglike activities. Things seem solid and the no-thing seems to be in danger today. Man cannot live without love in all of its many forms (brotherly love, erotic love, agapeistic love, love of children, love of God) and yet these seem to be giving way to dehumanizing substitutes. Love relationships show signs of becoming different forms of commodity exchange. Man who produces things can, if he lets himself, become nothing but a superconsumer. He can come to experience himself in economic terms. His life can become a thing which must be carefully invested in order to bring him maximum profit. Feelings of dissatisfaction, loss, guilt, or shame are overcome by buying some thing. Marriage becomes the "best deal" possible on the acquisition of a lifetime partner. Sex, like any business venture, hinges on the development of the proper technology. (The right technology is the only thing separating the successful from the unsuccessful lover.) Love, like every economic enterprise, is an exercise in teamwork and (sex) consumption.

A serious question can be asked about the very possibility of love understood as self-giving in a society dominated not by giving but by getting and saving. Can a society dominated by the mechanism of exchanging and saving promote, indeed permit, love? Not only is there overwhelming evidence of the decline of all forms of love in our society, but there are thinkers (e.g., R. D. Laing, the English psychiatrist) who argue an incompatibility between love and life as it is organized in contemporary society. They claim that our society and its dominant institutions, especially its economic institutions, form people in opposite directions from love. Not love, but competition with the other is promoted; not self-giving, concern, respect, but consumption, exploitation, and a veneer of respect hiding a deep aggressiveness. Only a saint can be a lover in such a condition. Love can survive only as a result of a revolution or a reformation, because the principles of a commercial society are the opposite of the principles of love. A person in the professions, a doctor, a chemist, a teacher, might presumably have sufficient distance from the influence of economic institutions to make love possible despite social influences, but what about those men intimately involved with the dominant cultural forces —the salesmen, the managers, the workers? Can a loving attitude be developed in someone whose life is involved deeply with the production-oriented, thing-centered, commodity- and consumer-directed Establishment? Does not love in such a circumstance inevitably fall into some commercial distortion of love? Can love, in a thoroughly commercial, thing-dominated society, be anything more than a marginal phenomenon?

If love is an essential part of human life, then much more attention must be given to the conditions which make its appearance a possibility and its development a value. Lovers, rather than millionaires and movie stars, will have to become our cultural heroes. The great technology and the things which it produces will have to be put in their proper places. At least we know they are not God. That's a start. If love is a sharing and a self-giving, then something of this must be possible even in our work and day-to-day activities. Man should not have to repress or destroy something so central to human fulfillment in order to make a living. To the degree to which the institutions of our culture inhibit or repress the possibility of love, to that degree they are immoral and cry for reform. Love in the sense of romantic love can only be present on an interpersonal level, but love in a broader sense of concern, respect, responsibility for the other must be a social, even economic phenomenon. To become a lover in this broader sense requires an uncommon act of courage.

Part 3

The God Question

There is an intimate relationship between a philosophy of human existence and the question of God. This has always been the case because one of the aspects of human behavior which separates man from the beast is his preoccupation with God and his practice of religion. Serious philosophers have always addressed themselves to the God question and consequently the history of philosophy is full of reflection and argumentation about religion. What has always been the case is even more so today. In our time the link between serious reflection on human existence and thought about God's existence is stronger than ever. The great contemporary philosophers who have made human existence the subject matter of their thought have been forced into consideration of the God question. Some, like Nietzsche and Freud, were militant atheists but both dedicated many pages and sizable intellectual energy to grappling with the God-man question. Kierkegaard's one theme and single passion was the relationship between human existence and religious faith.

The God question is inextricably bound to serious thought about contemporary human existence because the central fact of contemporary history has been the decline of belief. For Western man, before our age, God was the sun around which his existence revolved. God's existence provided not just the foundation of every system of meaning and values but perhaps more importantly a context of psychological warmth in which man lived out his daily life. The disappearance of this sun and center for many people, and the decline in its importance for most, has had serious effects upon contemporary man's experience. The life of contemporary man is experienced so differently from that of his ancestors that it is more than justified to speak of our time as the beginning of a new historical stage—perhaps even a new stage of human evolution.

God for medieval man was more than an intellectual category. God's existence and his relationship to man provided a psychological matrix in which man lived and died. God was not only the explanation of the universe but also the sanctifier of every important event in the individual's life: birth—baptism, maturity—confirmation, nourishment—eucharist, reconciliation —penance, life choice—matrimony or Holy Orders, death— extreme unction. The decline of God or the loss of belief in God seriously affected the very center of man's being. Nietzsche, who welcomed the death of God, nonetheless recognized the serious human crisis which this caused. If Nietzsche could not become the Messiah of the new historical period he saw man's fate as nihilism and self-destruction. For Kierkegaard the only question worthy of the serious philosophers was whether or not it was possible for contemporary man to live the Christian life. Is human existence enhanced by the disappearance of God, or a decline in the place of God in human life? Is it the case that man's involvement with God was just another illusion of a primitive period of his history? In comparison with this question the topics of logic and language which preoccupy the "professional philosophers" seem peripheral if not inane.

Chapter 8

Religion and Contemporary Culture

Changes in culture and the effects of these on the quality of human life are very difficult to pinpoint. Such an enterprise is comparable to articulating in conceptual categories the ever-elusive *Zeitgeit*. More often than not we become aware of a cultural turn only after it has taken place. Just as law lags behind societal change, understanding of the significant developments in a culture lags behind the developments. Being attuned to history is one way of keeping track of the direction of change. A complete history of the contemporary cultural situation certainly does not belong in a book of this sort, and yet some type of background awareness of how the present crisis came to be is a necessary precondition for finding a way out of it. Since in this final section we will be interested in the question of the relationship between human existence and God, we will begin with a short historical sketch of those steps which led Western civilization away from religious roots and experience into secularity.

Science and the Making of a Secular Culture

The best way to trace the decline of religious belief in contemporary life is to look at the beginnings of science. Copernicus, for example, was a revolutionary figure in more ways than one.

Not only did he reverse the relationship between the earth and the sun; he also changed the way human beings thought about themselves. All of us today are heirs of both these Copernican revolutions.

The pre-Copernican man considered the earth to be the center of the universe and thought of both as having been created for himself alone. The moon, sun, stars, and planets all revolved around the earth for man's benefit, i.e., so that he might see and testify to the glory of God who had arranged this spectacular. The God who watched over the heavens watched over medieval man as well. God recorded man's good and evil acts and finally crowned his earthly existence with salvation (if the final tally came out in the black).

Pre-Copernican man "knew his place" and it was a grandiose one. Man was at the center of the universe. He was the apex of a marvelous creation. If this were not enough, he was further elevated to divine sonship and a position as heir to eternal life. The universe was seen as a background symbol of man's exalted position. The order, harmony, and consistency between the natural world and the world of the spirit permeated medieval man's life with meaning.

All this man was sure of because God himself had revealed these truths. God was a *mysterium tremendum*, and as such filled man with awe and anxiety. But on the other hand, God had arranged the whole natural order for man and if that were not enough, God revealed to man the central truths about his existence and drew close to him in an intimate Father-Son relationship. Man's life then was a combination of awesome mystery and clear understanding. Mystery surrounded the making of the heavens, the earth, and human life itself. It seemed reasonable that man live surrounded by such impenetrable mystery because man and everything which made up his world were the result of an unfathomable creation. Everywhere he turned medieval man confronted mystery, but the mysteries fell together into an altogether logical and comprehensible pattern created by revelation and theology.

The development of science changed all this. The great scientists pushed back the veil of incomprehension. With the development of science came the gradual disappearance of one mystery after another, and finally the very disappearance of the supreme mystery—God. Science increased man's understanding but dislodged him both from his presumed place at the center of things and from the system of theological beliefs which gave his life such deep significance.

Copernicus first, then Kepler and Galileo, and still later Newton, changed both the image of the universe and the image of man's place in it. The earth, rather than being the center of things, became a small planet revolving around a much larger sun. Both earth and sun were shown to form part of a larger galaxy which may contain as many as a hundred million planetary systems. There are other galaxies, too, besides our own— as many as one billion. All these planets and galaxies together are like tiny particles in an infinite ocean of space. What once appeared as a marvelous and mysterious display of God's creativity, arranged for man's edification and with man's world (earth) at the very center, science looked at differently. Both man and earth were dislodged from center stage.

The only thing that remained of the older system after the Copernican revolution had fully evolved was the mystery of life. Science might explain the movement of the planets but could not explain the emergence of man. Man, the animal who knows, is aware, is capable of conceptualizing, understanding, dominating the world, is separate from the world. He stands apart from all the rest and remains impermeable even to the sharp gaze of science. Or so it seemed until science turned to man.

Darwin and biologists tended to do for human life what the cosmologists had done for the earth and other planets. Darwin discovered the "law of gravity" for the science of man. He showed us conclusively that man did not come ready-made from the hand of God, but rather passed through many inferior forms and structures before emerging as *homo sapiens*. Every living creature was in a sense man's ancestor. Man evolved from lower species and then developed a unique way of handling the environment, which we call culture. Adaptation and survival of the fittest were the principles of development. Darwin pushed back the veil of mystery surrounding man's origin and his relationship to other living creatures.

Radical changes in man's image of himself accompanied the development of the physical and biological sciences. Rather than being the apex of creation and the reason why everything else in the universe existed, man began to see himself as a tiny cosmic accident. It made no sense to think of himself as "a little less than the angels" because angels had become myths. Even God, who once was the center around which everything revolved, gradually became a "superfluous hypothesis." Copernicus was a religious man. So were Kepler, Galileo, Newton, and Darwin. Each tried to hold on to his religion. Accompanying every new scientific treatise, strong statements testifying to faith were made. As science became more sure of its hypotheses, however, scientists became more bold in their philosophies. When Napoleon asked Pierre Laplace (who was explaining how the world came to be) where God fits into the picture, he received the straightforward answer of a man inflated with the competency of his ideas. "*Sire, je n'avais besoin de cette hypothèse.*"[1] Eighteenth-century Deists retained the God concept but reduced the being described by this term to an original creator and lawgiver who subsequently had nothing to do with his production. When, however, all types of "flaws" and "imperfections" in the system were discovered, even the Deists' God fell from his place as all-wise creator.

Science developed a method for arriving at truth which became increasingly more effective in handling the world and gradually surrounded itself with an enormous prestige. It started with a presupposition that reality was physical, and then devised efficient ways of measuring it. The measuring devices which scientists developed came to be the standards of what is real. What *really* exists is what can be measured and verified by

1. The story seems to have many different forms. The above version is listed in *The Macmillan Book of Proverbs, Maxims, and Famous Phrases*, p. 107.

scientific instruments. The success of the measuring techniques and the control over nature which these techniques generated gave to scientific knowledge an air of infallibility. From being a *certain* form of knowing it was a small step to consider science the *only* form of knowing. Whatever did not fall within the parameters of the scientific method first became suspect and then was outrightly denied existence. If a presumed reality could not be verified by the scientific method it was considered a myth or a superstition. Such was the fate of "realities" like value or justice (in the ethical world), universals and transcendentals (in the philosophical world), and then statements about origins and ultimate ends which included all types of religious beliefs. God himself finally fell victim to the new method of knowing.

Scientific experiments generated data (in the sense of verified bits of information) which were expressed in the language of mathematics. Laws in turn were developed out of the data which explained the functioning of measured reality. The laws of science gradually pushed back man's ignorance by explaining many of the phenomena which previously were considered mysterious. The scientists hypothesized about all the laws being interrelated and expressible in one giant formula which would encompass all lesser explanations. Science indeed aspired after total understanding. The God who in medieval times seemed to be working everywhere in the universe fell more and more into the background. Scientific man saw only the operation of "natural" laws. No longer did he stand in awe before the phenomena of life and the world. The new man was confident of knowning how and why everything happened in this or that way. Whereas once man approached reality with a sense of mystery, the scientifically trained person approached it with only his instruments of measurement. The advance of science was accompanied by the decline in a sense of mystery, belief in God, and religious practice.

Evolution is a good example of a scientific hypothesis displacing a religious belief. The concept is identified in the popular mind with Darwin but actually it preceded him by centuries.[1] Modern science showed again and again that everything evolved and actually continues yet in a state of evolution. Evolution became the law governing both planets and man. Its explanations seemed adequate without any reference to God.

Interestingly enough, however, the same theory of evolution which initially seemed to displace God, in a more mature formulation, raises questions which seem to reintroduce the God possibility. Most evolutionists concentrate on what has already taken place: the few thousand years of recorded history; the millions of years of human development; the billions of years when the universe evolved without either life or man. We know something about the long road that led to man: the emergence of living from nonliving matter; the emergence of man from the animals. These were the great events of an evolution that has taken place. Is there another great event toward which man and evolution are moving that will qualitatively change him and move the process on to an even higher plane? What is the next stage? Where is man going? What is going to happen now that man is in charge of evolution?

When man gained control of evolution by discovering its laws, evolution became conscious of itself. Man has now quite literally made himself in the image of God, by gathering in his own hands the power to mold his destiny. The power put in man's hands by science makes old questions about the source and finality of human life more urgent. Does human life have some transcendent value or is it as violable as anything else—an accident which came to be by chance and now drifts toward extinction either by its own hand or by the chaos in which it is immersed?

It certainly cannot be proven with "scientific" data, but it does seem reasonable to entertain a different hypothesis, i.e., that evolution had its cosmological phase; then later a biological era; then entered the age of conscious reflection. The process reflects a certain order and each element has played a role in the

---

1. The concept was held by different pre-Socratic philosophers. Anaximander believed that higher forms of life evolved from lower and that the sea was the origin of the development. Empedocles held a version of natural selection.

program. This hypothesis suggests a further question: whose program is this? Does the development of science, which seemed in the early stages to make God an unnecessary hypothesis, in a more mature period actually pose the God problem with even more forcefulness? If evolution has progressed to where man now can understand and control it, then some notion of the aim and purpose of this great enterprise is urgently needed. Nothing is more fearful than power joined to ignorance. The issue at stake is the future of man and the quality of every individual life. Does man live just to carry on an absurd accident or is man called to join with one who intended him originally, in the construction of an even higher form of human life?

The urgency of these questions is increased by the record of man's tenure in the office of steward or manager of the evolutionary process. In the relatively few short years of man's control, disruptions of every sort have occurred. The environment which contributed to the development of life and supported it has in many areas become a stagnant cesspool. Rivers which support no fish have come to be. Air in which no bird can fly has invaded the atmosphere. Human beings, rather than moving toward an ever higher form of consciousness and love, are in alarming numbers becoming incapable of either reflection or caring. Man, the caretaker, has begun his tenure by developing not power to care for or to cure, but power to destroy not only himself but even the earth from which he sprang. Our crisis is our own. There is no way to drift and still survive. Man has to step out to meet the situation he created. This means he has to do some serious thinking about himself. What is man? In what is he different from lower forms? How best can his unique features be preserved and developed? After spending so much time and energy thinking about how to dominate the earth and make it his own, man now has to think about his own life and how to keep it from being something he suffers and endures rather than develops and enjoys.

Contemporary man traces his beginning to the development of science and technology. The history of science and technology is the history of contemporary man and contemporary culture. One very important development associated with this history of events has been the gradual yet real disappearance of religion. Contemporary man is secular. Ours is the only culture in history without a God-experience. In the enthusiasm which surrounded the beginnings of science "enlightened man" made his self-assured statement, *"Je n'avais besoin de cette hypothèse."* Given the record of man's tenure in the role of God, can we make that statement today with the same assurance and certainty? One need be neither a prophet of doom nor neurotically maudlin to be pessimistic about man's survival. Man has to change in order to survive. There is a real chance that he will do neither. There is on the other hand no chance of abandoning science and technology. Man cannot go back. And yet he needs to make an ethical leap corresponding to the jump he took with the development of science in order to hope for a better tomorrow. Is it possible that the ethical poverty which threatens his existence could be related to his precipitous abandonment of God? Could the power to make this next ethical leap come only from God?

Besides being a physical, spiritual, ethical, social being, it might just be the case that man is also a religious being. One of the aspects of man's uniqueness could be an openness to God and a vocation to divine relationship. If so, rejection of God would be as destructive to his humanness as the rejection of any one of his other unique possibilities. If man does not face up to his physical or biological being he courts destruction. The same is so of his capacity to search for meaning, or to make choices, or to enter deep intimate relationships. Does the structure of man include both a capacity and a call to religious experience such that without this man becomes crippled? The rejection or repression of any one of man's possibilities immediately affects all the rest of his being. The various levels of the human structure are different enough to be separately defined but they do not exist in isolation one from the other. For example, a refusal to choose or commit oneself (ethical) inevitably affects man's capacity for relationship (social) and his search for meaning (spiritual). If man is also a religious being then the loss of his religious potentiality will cause the whole of his being to suffer maladjustment.

Given the precarious situation of human life, it makes sense to reconsider the religious question. Was the abandonment of God and religion a necessary concomitant to the development of science? Or did man throw out too much? Was his enthusiasm for scientific knowledge exaggerated? Are there good reasons why cultures before our own were religious? Is primitive man all that primitive? Are we all that advanced? The concern of this last section will be with the question of man and religion.

Philosophy and the Return of Religious Concern

Human experience indicates that the world has patterns or structures which can be both understood and increasingly better understood. Deepening understanding brings power and a corresponding degree of control over the future. Man has always been scientific to a degree but only recently has a method for this type of knowing been refined to produce more information than anyone is able to assimilate. Scientific knowing is open-ended in the sense that more experimentation can either further refine or perhaps radically change what is known. Contrary to common opinion, scientific knowing is tentative. It is future-oriented in the sense that it requires further justification.

Another type of knowing that grows out of the same base of experience is called philosophy, or philosophical anthropology. It too is a reflection upon understandable experience with an eye toward deepening insight into that peculiar center of experience—the human person. Philosophy centering on the individual existent is a different type of knowing because the human person is not like any thing and is not amenable to the methodology designed to understand things. After doing every conceivable scientific test we still do not understand Paul of Tarsus or Joan of Arc—or even Jim Smith or Betty Jones. Human experience is the experience of a unique individual. Each and every human experience invites reflection and further understanding. Some experiences are trivial or evanescent. Others are crucial and of lasting import. The wise man knows how to distinguish between them. He also knows how to analyze and deepen understanding of himself. His knowledge is different from that of the scientist but it is nonetheless true knowledge. Some would say it is the highest form of knowledge—wisdom.

People today, especially those whom we would call the managerial class—those who are responsible for the day-to-day operation of our culture—are almost exclusively involved with scientific or practical knowing. They have to understand the world outside. They have to know how it operates and how they must control it for maximum benefit. Their concerns are with things and processes. Knowledge of this sort paradoxically can destroy man rather than guarantee his survival. Reflection directed to only one pole of existence (that which is outside man) can destroy a very delicate balance between subject and object. Man must also be concerned about himself. He must pursue an ever more adequate understanding of the mysterious being that he is. It is not enough to know what is outside. Man must know himself. He must learn to appreciate the human. He must develop sensitivities for central or crucial human experience and not confuse these with the trivial. Only the wise man can avoid the fate of him who possesses all *things* and "suffers the loss of his soul."

And yet it is a matter of fact that the American culture is permeated with a preference for the "outside" or the objective. Americans generally are pragmatists who want to know how things work or how to make things work even better. Questions about the human person, or the mystery of being, tend to put them off. For the typical American there is just too much to be done. Time spent on what we have described as philosophical questions appears to be a waste of time. Doing, producing, changing, improving, testing—these are *real* activities in contrast to meditation or reflection upon life. Those who engage in these latter activities are like those who write poetry or listen to classical music. They are just a little "kookie." Any mention of the problem of God or evil or authentic existence creates suspicion. "What is he—a hippie?" And yet can a reasonable man, in whatever culture, preoccupy himself exclusively with one type of activity (the practical or scientific) to the exclusion of another (the more personalistic or the philosophical)? Can a reasonable man just do things without asking whether his works are of value? How can we distinguish what is valuable from what is not, without serious thought about what enhances the human and what does not? Can man avoid being at least mildly philosophical?[1]

It is unavoidable that a great part of our life is taken up with survival. We are simply forced to learn to understand the operation of things and ultimately how to control them. The American preference for the practical is not all wrong. It is, however, lopsided. The manager, the scientist, the engineer, and the administrator are also *human* beings. Each is filled with fears and hopes, anxieties and aspirations. All these are experiences which stand in need of analysis and interpretation. To use one's human life as if it were an instrument for doing other things is a tragedy. Human life is not an instrumental but an intrinsic value.

Our concern in this section will be to attempt to analyze human experience in such a way as to show in it the foundation of a serious reconsideration of God and religion. There is little doubt that the development of science and practical knowing has pushed aside religion. Can another look at man's experience reverse the slide toward secularization? Can a revival of an old-fashioned philosophy, concerned with the human, help us refocus and see in our finite selves a pointer to the infinite?

Any suggestion of reopening the religious question is met with one very substantial obstacle. How can contemporary man, whose experience has for so long excluded God, approach the subject? Certainly he cannot be expected to become a reader of religious books on command. Where can he plug into the ques-

---

1. Only Americans can reconcile *giving* money to the churches on the basis of whatever practical effects these institutions may have on the community without giving any serious thought to the philosophical question: whether we are alone in empty space or in the presence of a creator who addresses us in the events of our personal lives and in history.

tion? Religion, which once was so natural, has become an enigma. God and religious experience were once man's daily bread. His religious convictions were so strong that he confused disbelief with insanity. Now the world of religion seems strange and "religious experience" is a phrase which generates neither meaning nor passion. The prevailing attitude of contemporary man toward religion is indifference rather than passion. Certainly religion is no longer something to fight about. Without a religious experience of his own to fall back upon, contemporary man tends to identify religion with another age and another experience. Stepping into church is like going into another world, an older one, strange to the full-fledged inhabitant of a scientific age. People who are "into religion" are presumed to be either antimodern or ignorant of the intellectual framework in which contemporary life takes place. Can a move toward philosophy which helps man refocus on his less objective lived experience at least reintroduce the religious question and make religious concern culturally acceptable?

Secularism or Religion

The process by which Western man moved from an experience shot through with the religious to one in which the religious has become strange and enigmatic is called *secularization*. For some the term is synonymous with progress. *Secular* for these is another way of saying sensible, reasonable, progressive. Secularity is a commitment to this world, which is assumed to be the only one that exists in fact. Religion as a preoccupation with yet another world is judged a "sinful" waste of time. Those who waste time on such pursuits are backward or stupid. The secularists "thank God" that our age has been the first in man's history which moved away from concern with the transcendent and dedicated itself to the improvement of the "real" world of everyday life.

Before beginning to evaluate the antireligious or a-religious aspect of the secularization process it is worth remembering that nothing is completely black or white. However one comes out on the question of whether secularization in its core sense (worldly as opposed to religious) is an advance or a disastrous impoverishment of human experience, it is hardly arguable that a great deal of what has been accomplished in the process is good. The development of advanced technology and industrialization is not synonymous with evil. These developments have brought benefits to man. Control over nature has made it possible to place a human stamp on the environment rather than be exposed to its always dangerous changes. In some cases, however, this new power has been used demonically. Instead of using power to cultivate and bring nature to fullest human benefit, man has used scientific-technological power to exploit and destroy both nature and himself. We have already made reference to this and it is too obvious for further comment. The point is that secularization is a mixed bag, a combination of good and evil. It is one thing to understand that the process has taken place. It is another thing to interpret it. The difficulty is to distinguish the good from the evil.

There is widespread agreement on one point. Secular man is more autonomous than his predecessor. Power and control over nature have brought a degree of independence from its arbitrariness. In the degree to which man's reason and freedom were enhanced in the development of science and technology, to that degree man demanded more respect. Man's control over nature made him more aware of himself as autonomous. As this heightened experience of his independence and power spread, demands swelled for political changes which respect these qualities. It is the worst form of inconsistency to be free from subjection to natural arbitrariness and still subject to the political whims of an absolute monarch. The French Revolution cannot be dissociated from the scientific revolution of the same eighteenth century. Science gave man a new way of reasoning. Technology gave him new powers and control. A more rational and freer being demands to be treated as such, which means to have the right to think for himself and freely express his will. No longer subject to nature, man insisted on not being subject to any absolute authority. Kings fell throughout Europe to be replaced by some form of democratic representative government. Scientific-technological-industrial-secular culture developed a more autonomous man and a freer society.[1]

The negative side of this good is a modern sickness called individualism. Many a modern secular man has moved beyond a heightened awareness of his independence or autonomy into a stance of independence and separateness from everyone and everything. Rather than being a rational and free being in community with other free and rational beings, many a secular man thinks and acts as a wolf in a world of dog-eat-dog. One simply cannot at one and the same time "do his own thing" and create human community. Autonomy has become extreme individualism, which translated in action means an unconcerned and uncaring attitude toward other human beings. A disintegration of community has accompanied secular man's autonomy and independence. Secular man dwells in cities which have become ant hills of *private* persons. Anonymity has grown up alongside autonomy. One almost has to go back to the small towns with strong religious traditions to find real human community.

Another change accompanying the secularization process is a new emphasis on the here-and-now. In religious times the here-and-now was experienced against the backdrop of eternity. What was seen and felt witnessed to what was unseen and felt only at privileged moments. The temporal order was important for religious people but not as important as the eternal. The *really real* for them was that which was beyond temporal processes. What is seen, they felt, will pass away but what transcends this order remains fixed and unchangeable. Critics of

---

1. Paradoxically, the same culture seems to be taking away what first it granted as a gift. Increasingly, secular man worries about his freedom and his autonomy. There is no dearth of talk about freedom but man feels less and less free. He seems to be losing the power to control his life, without which freedom is pure rhetoric.

religious man and human life in times of religious emphasis have objected to the distraction created by the eternal or the transcendent. The most telling objection to religious belief in this century is one that accuses religion of holding back temporal progress. Too much time presumably is wasted on what does not contribute to man's building up of this earth. Believers are considered deficient human beings and bad citizens. Nietzsche was the most outspoken advocate of the new secular ideal. Atheism for him was the key to rebuilding the earth and making man a superman. Religious faith condemned man to weakness and the earth to stagnation.

Secular man has an impressive record to support his contention of being "true to this earth." Although there is suspicion afoot that the new earth and the new man amount to a misbegotten venture, there is no denying that they are the work of man dedicated to the earth. No transcendent concern distracted his attention from the here-and-now. The temporal displaced the eternal. Time became identified with the present—the immediate reality. Not only did the eternal disappear but even the past seemed unworthy of attention. The future was unknown and unpredictable. This left the present moment to bear the whole burden of human life. Secularization, by eliminating the eternal backdrop for temporal existence, gradually created a passion for the only time left—the present.

One important result of the new secular sense of time has been a gradual erosion of interest in long-term projects. Interest is aroused by what is *now*—or by what promises immediate results. There is little tolerance for what requires long-term loyalty and devotion. Disappointment or displeasure are likely to precipitate quick withdrawal.

Changes in sex behavior and marriage offer a wealth of good examples of this development. Marriage was once a lifelong commitment and sex was a sign of lifelong fidelity and love. There was little doubt that marriage involved disappointments, displeasures, restrictions, and obligations. The marriage ceremony and the social morality hammered home the note of commitment in face of great disappointment and difficulty. ("For better or worse, for richer or poorer.") Sex was a powerful symbol of commitment and associated both with loyalty and fidelity. Undoubtedly the burdens, the obligations, and the restrictions associated with sexuality were overplayed. Little was heard or said about sensuality as good, sex as play, spontaneity or joy in relationship. Nowadays the tables are turned. Sex is just play, a "now thing." It is spontaneous to the point of doing away with even such "formalities" as an introduction of the participating persons. If something feels good, the new morality says *do it*. Secularized sex is freer and uncomplicated by implied commitments.

Marriage too is no longer so long-range. It is now a temporary and disposable relationship. "When either one of us gets tired or 'feels hassled'—we split." The new styles of sex and marriage are symbolic of life in a secular era. Certainly the development is not all bad and yet one cannot avoid the impression that something substantial and crucial to life has been lost. Great art, no less than successful and fulfilling human relationships, demands sacrifice, discipline, endurance, and suffering. Neither is possible where the emphasis is on the immediate, here-and-now enjoyment.

Goals, ideals, projects give to human life a unity and continuity important for fulfillment. Without these life is exhausted in one isolated now after another. Commitment to not-yet-realized goals creates a continuity of action. Without continuity, life has neither stages nor purposive development but only disconnected experiences. Secular life creates the impression of being dribbled away rather than being ordered and organized by something real which is beyond the present. Elimination of the not yet, the hoped for, the eternal, or concentration on the here-and-now, did create the conditions for rebuilding the earth. Secularity took the present seriously and worked at it assiduously. In the process, however, it also seems to have flattened the experience of time and impoverished human existence. Life conceived as a disconnected series of moments is poor in comparison to life lived in relationship to the not yet, the hoped for, the eternal. God working in and through history gave the past great significance and filled the future with hope. Religion gave greater depth and breadth to human existence. It made possible an optimism even in the face of disappointment. Since God created life, it was good. Celebration was possible because God's presence constituted an enduring promise. Good rather than evil will ultimately triumph. The here-and-now is important for the believer but it does not bear the whole weight of existence. Since man is not alone but in partnership with God he need not be so pressed down with the way things are.

After all his doing and experiencing, secular man tends to suffer despair. Without the unifying effect on personality, the continuity of life, and the identity created by an absolute commitment to God, many secular men (usually at about forty) look back over life and wonder, who am I? who is the real me? As the here-and-nows become less fascinating, spontaneous, and immediately rewarding, why put up with them? Males especially are the victims of this development. They seem to have swallowed secular life and climbed aboard secularity as a whole generation of Germans climbed aboard Nazism.[1]

The point of this section is not to condemn secularity or secular existence but rather to suggest that like all else in life, religion included, it has both positive and negative consequences for human existence. We have already mentioned the tendency of religion to ignore or to give less than enthusiastic attention to this world and the present. If our topic were the deficiencies of traditional religious life styles we might add a mention of the many instances of ethical insensitivity which seem peculiar to believers (e.g., *no* to abortion but *go* to war— *yes* to charity but *no* to economic equality for the disadvantaged). Good is never totally identifiable with one style and evil with another. Alongside the deficiencies associated with secular-

---

1. Excepting the radical feminists who want to imitate male existence in its most dehumanizing forms, women have kept a distance from the new attitudes. They continue to value commitment, loyalty, fidelity, and the rest. Given the trauma which males today suffer around age forty, female menopause has become pale and insignificant.

ity one notices the unique positive contributions made to human life in general and even, oddly enough, to religion.

The attention given by secular man to this world is a reminder to Judeo-Christian believers that God created the world and saw that it was good. In the Biblical tradition, world, time, history are all creations of God and man is called to bring them to fulfillment. The Judeo-Christian religion rejected the view that the world is evil. If nature, the world, the present, the sensible, indeed even the sensuous bear witness to God who made them good, then involvement with them cannot be evil. Autonomy and independence do not constitute sin but a coming to maturity—the development of potentiality put in man by God. The criticisms of religion voiced by exponents of secularity witness to failures which religion must confront if it is to survive. As a matter of fact, religion has not kept pace with much of modern development (either intellectual or institutional). Religious authority has been heavy-handed and unconvincing. Neither Christianity nor Judaism, however, collapses under criticism. Secular criticism has performed a service which religion can hardly afford to dispense with.

If secularity witnesses to a part of the truth, cannot the same be said for religion? If religion is benefitted by the perspective of the secularist, cannot the tables be turned with profit? Is not secular life also open to criticism? Does anyone disagree with the idea that contemporary secular life suffers from narrowness, boredom—dehumanizations of all sorts? Could a total exclusion of religion from life be as much a mistake as a flat religious condemnation of secularity? Truth does not lie on one or another side of competing claims because truth is never identifiable with the incomplete. Each conflicting position needs the perspective of the other. Is it reasonable to think that truth is totally on the religious side or entirely on the side of secularity? The criticisms each make of the other have validity. Each position is a combination of light and darkness, success and failure. Admitting this, can we avoid interpreting the complete exclusion of God and religion as a loss? If it makes sense at least to consider the questions of God and religion seriously, then where do we look for indications which a reasonable secular man might accept that human existence is among other things an openness to relationship with God? This last question brings us to our final topic—a search for a religious dimension in the structure of human experience.

Chapter 9

Religion and Human Experience

There was a time when God and religion were closely tied to the world. Medieval thinkers searched the world for data which might be interpreted as pointing to God. Thomas Aquinas had one specifically cosmological proof for God but all his "proofs" were cosmological in the sense that they began reflection with some aspect of the world (change, design, etc.). It was typical of medieval man to see nature as the clearest reflection of God's existence. The world of nature was interpreted religiously to such an extent that almost every natural thing symbolized a religious reality. Protestantism stripped away this religious symbolism because of the danger of confusing symbol with reality, leaving man as the only "natural" phenomenon which continued to point to God. Contemporary Americans are heirs of the Protestant Reformation. The world for us is bare, seen only in terms of efficient and material causality. It is devoid of religious significance and no longer "speaks" to us of God.

Human Experience and Its Interpretations

Given the situation of contemporary man, the only foundation on which to build a case for God and religion is *human experience*. If we can find in man's interpreted experience of himself and others traces of God, then a case can be made for secular man's reconsideration of religion. If we cannot find in human experience any trace of God or rumor of angel, then religious belief will be without rational justification. The questions of God and religious belief are intertwined then with the question of man. A decision whether or not to give serious consideration to the religious question hinges on an anterior consideration of human experience, its structure, purpose, goal, etc. God and man are bound together at least in a philosophy of experience.

Human experience like the world in which it is immersed presents us with a paradox. On the surface it seems diaphanous and decipherable. We all have the impression that we understand ourselves and have a reasonable grasp of the outside world. Upon closer observation, however, the presumed clarity disappears. Human nature and the physical world are steeped in secrets which disclose themselves only to the patient and persistent observer. It is altogether possible for us to think we understand, only to find out we have been cultivating an illusion. The complexities of human experience are as much in need of careful analysis as the atoms or molecules which preoccupy so many scientific minds. If careful and reasonable analysis supports an interpretation which points to God, then perhaps even secular man can recover that lost dimension of his existence. If on the other hand human experience like Pascal's universe shows us only silence and darkness, then we can resign ourselves to going it alone in life. We can consider ourselves freed from the gnawing suspicion that we are neglecting the Being who holds the key to human fulfillment.

Human experience is not something that happens "within" a subject. Rather it is an interaction between a self-conscious being and a multifaceted reality beyond the self. The conditions for the possibility of experience include a being which is structured such as to be capable of encountering, taking note of, and then responding to something beyond itself. The something else which the experiencing subject confronts is stable, reliable, and more than the subject's mental image, e.g., a person, an object, an event. The outside something is related to the conscious subject by reason of the subject's correlative receptor system.

The outside has its own separate tenure and so does the experiencing subject. And yet they are capable of contact and interaction. It is only common sense that the object or the person outside makes a difference in experience. Not quite so immediately evident but just as obvious upon closer examination is the fact that the structure of the subject experiencing also makes a difference. There is then a certain asymmetry as well as a certain symmetry which exists between the person experiencing and the reality experienced.

Because experience embodies an interaction between an objective and a subjective pole, the problem of defining the exact limit of each component is unavoidable. What exactly belongs to the self who encounters and what is "really there" for encountering? There are other problems. The object, person, or event encountered is never fully revealed. The "outside" has both a surface and a depth. The simplest reality is capable of constituting the life project of a great mind and still its depth will never be sounded. The same is so of the subject. Experience is so rich and varied that it resists both completion and reduction to either one or another pole.

Not only does reality offer deeper and more superficial levels but one passes from one to another level by means of interpretation. All experience requires interpretation. When man moves beyond the most prosaic statements about the simplest experience (e.g., "the broom is in the corner") room is opened up for differing interpretations. Science is one form of interpretation, one which has its own special interests and which uses its own abstract categories of number, shape, position, etc. Philosophy is another form of interpretation manifesting different interests and different methods of explanation. Religion is yet another form of interpretation, with its peculiar interests and method. The interpreted experience is in need of critical support. It is not sufficient to say that I interpret such and such an experience in this or that way. An argument of some sort must be made to support a proposed interpretation. Science offers its arguments; so, too, does philosophy. If it is legitimate to speak of a religious interpretation of experience, then it too must be made intelligible. When an experience is interpreted as pointing to

God or when God is proposed as the ground of existence, the link between my surface experience and an interpretation of its deeper levels must be explicated. Showing just how certain human experiences suggest the question of God is one way of stating the goal of this final section.

Although direct experience of the surface of reality certainly does not point to God, it can be argued that an analysis of the deeper levels of reality does. When we encounter an orange tree we can stop and say, "Oh, there's an orange tree!" Or we can look more deeply and consider it in terms of its economic values, the price of its fruit, its productivity, etc. We could encounter it as a historic object, one having a certain age, and incorporating the pruning activities of many generations of men. If we were more aesthetic than economic or historical we might encounter it as a thing of beauty and merely let it be before us and appreciate it. Finally, we could encounter it as a marvelous work, which speaks to us of purpose, intention, meaning, all of which suggest the possibility of an intending, meaningful, purposeful creator.

Objects and persons are such that they lend themselves to many different types of encounter and correspondingly many different types of experience. The human self is such that it can have interest in one or more aspects of outside reality. Man is spatio-temporal, economic, historical, aesthetic, *and religious.* Reflection upon man's encounter with the world can lead to his posing the question of God. It can be argued then that human experience has a religious dimension, understanding by that statement a posing of the God question which comes from an analysis of the deeper dimensions of either the subjective or objective poles of experience. We might ask, for example, about the conditions for the possibility of there being something rather than nothing. We might inquire about the possibility of an intelligent source for a human existence which is questioning. Not every object, person, or event encountered will as a matter of fact suggest a religious perspective, but every experience could do so.

For example, the human person is capable of pulling the spiritual world or the world of meanings together into a whole

—a cosmos. Through imagination and by use of conceptual categories man can envisage the whole of existence and then ask if this whole has a meaning and a purpose. Not only is man capable of this type of relationship with reality but he has a propensity, an inclination to such behavior. The question of a final purpose or meaningfulness of the whole of existence is not a matter of indifference for man. Unless his natural curiosity has been suppressed, man has a strong interest in this type of question. To question why there is being rather than nonbeing, or to inquire into the possibility of an ultimate purposiveness, puts man into a religious mode. These are what we call religious questions. They put man in contact with the horizon of reality. They pose the question of a reality which, although lying beyond what is seen and heard, holds out the promise of integrating the dizzying complexity of experience into a satisfying synthesis. The fact that man both asks these questions naturally and has a vital interest in some sort of answer to them makes man an animal concerned with the ultimate.

That man before our culture had been religious is hardly a matter of argument. Religious practice, religious belief, religious experience are all part of man's history because man differs from other animals in that his existence alone has a religious dimension. His experience is such that it throws him into involvement with the ultimate horizon. Perhaps religion is old-fashioned, or the result of economic alienation (Marx), or a childish wish for a permanent father (Freud). But then again, perhaps religion is as natural to man as free choice, in which case its loss is itself an alienation from authentic human being.

The suggestion that man is naturally religious in the sense that his experience inevitably involves him with the God question might seem to some a tenuous proposition. Man asks questions about intelligent life in the universe but one would hardly argue from that that man is interstellar or has an interplanetary dimension. He might just as well display an interest in ghosts but little can be deduced from such behavior. There are some important differences, however, between the approach outlined above and those just-mentioned objections. In the first place man does not make merely theoretical inquiries about a possible absolute being. (Anyone might ask this type of question without considering himself religious.) Man inquires about an ultimate reality, a source of all that is, a final and necessary being, whom he names God. He moves from the theoretical possibility of an abstract being, or a force, to a concern about a personal being whom he calls God. Not only does he ask about God, but at the same time he asks about his own existence, its character, and its purpose. There is little religious significance in asking purely theoretical questions about the possibility of a prime mover but there is enormous religious significance in moving from this type of inquiry to ask about the existence of God. An abstract and theoretical inquiry into human being is very different from an inquiry which involves the purpose of my personal existence. Ultimate questioning justifies calling man religious if and only if it leads him to grapple existentially with the relationship between his life and God. If man does this naturally, then it makes sense to talk about a religious dimension to his experience. It even makes sense to speak of man as a religious animal.

The God Concept

Religion as we have been using the term means a relationship which holds between the experiencing self and the ultimate reality pointed to in experience. Religion is a discovery of the holy through interpretation, followed by all the many forms of communication through which persons interrelate. The ultimate reality can be differently described: reality beyond appearance; the depth of being; the richness or fullness of being; the power which keeps everything that is in existence; the power of being. The most common word used for these different expressions is God, and this term includes a suggestion of personhood.

God is a word used to express existence which is so full, rich, deep, powerful that it is undefinable in the most comprehensive concept. To speak about God in philosophy is to speak about that which goes beyond objects, events, persons, and yet appears in and through all these. God is "the personal more" which man is capable of "perceiving" in his experience of the world, himself, and other persons. God is the foundation of all that exists, the ideal which fulfills human nature, the goal toward which human beings aspire.

The concept of "God" is one that originates in some sort of experience. God is not a being generated by philosophical demonstration. Philosophy cannot prove either the existence or nonexistence of God. God cannot be purely a matter of logic. Either God is an integral part of human experience or he is not even worth arguing about. Philosophy plays an important role in religion but it is one that follows in both time and importance the actual religious experience or the religious interpretation of experience. Philosophy does not initiate religion; experience does. And yet without philosophy experience would lack logical structure. Philosophy reflects upon the experiences which seem to point beyond themselves to God. God's existence cannot be proven but philosophy can and does attempt to justify the God concept and give religious faith a rational foundation.

The religious object *God* is ordinarily not directly perceived. Man experiences what is not God. If the religious "object" is grasped at all it is in an interpretation of the nonreligious or the secular. The Absolute appears in the relative. The sacred shines through what is not sacred. The infinite is contacted in the finite. If the secular, the finite, the relative is collapsed into the sacred, we have idolatry. The religious "object" cannot be identified with that through which it appears. The constant message of the Old Testament is, "I am the Lord thy God, thou shalt not have strange Gods (idols) before me." If, on the other hand, the sacred is collapsed into the secular, the finite, and the relative, we have atheism. Atheism is the other side of idolatry. It is a looking at reality as appearance, and then making the interpretation, "That's all there is." Atheism is an interpretation characterized by a refusal to "go beyond." In a more positive sense atheism is a dedication to the world in the sense of the secular, the finite, and the relative. In Camus' phrase atheism is "being true to the earth."

Religion as dialogue with God has to be understood in relation to what it is not. It is a dialectical notion, requiring the opposite pole to be meaningful. The religious is opposed to the profane. Whatever can show forth the ultimate, point to the depth of being, witness to the power of being has a special importance for human life, because it can open up dialogue with God. What has no such potentiality is ordinary, or shallow, or profane. Special events, or objects, or persons, or relationships permit man to *see through*, to touch deeper levels of being. Touching deeper levels of being, however, is not equivalent to touching God. What man experiences is *not God* but nevertheless is *sacred* or religious, in the sense that it has the power to suggest God or point to a reality beyond this world. Human experience is not necessarily profane. This nonprofane experience we want to better understand.

Religious Experience, Direct and Indirect

A distinction must be made between this notion of religion, as contact with God through what is not God, and the concept of direct religious experiences, as used by many writers. In the first case religion came to be as a result of some special experience being interpreted as pointing to God. In the second it is a unique experience, or a peak experience, and is associated with a special feeling or a particular sense. Mysticism is the best example of such an exclusively religious experience. Such religious experience is the principal source of established religion and continues to nourish every vital religious tradition. (There are Catholic mystics, Protestant mystics, Jewish mystics, Moslem, Hindu, and Buddhist mystics.) Besides this direct experience, however, there is the potential of human experience which is not in itself directly religious indirectly pointing to the possibility of God and thereby becoming a medium of religion. Our methodology will center on this latter possibility.

Religious experience in the sense of direct religious experience holds an important place in religion but it is hardly a feasible approach to religion for secular man. In direct religious experience—or mystical experience—the reality of God or ultimate reality is *given* in an experience rather than being suggested or pointed to. The immediate experience of God carries with it its own interpretation. Like every experience, it requires interpretation but the interpretation is more forced than derived. The mystic has no problem identifying his experience as an experience of God. The problem arises when expression or communication is attempted. Some mystics simply conclude that what they experienced is ineffable and remain silent. Others resort to dialectical and contradictory expression (e.g., *Vivo sin vivir* of St. John of the Cross: "I live, but yet I do not live"). In any event, the interpretation of the experience as a God experience is evident and forceful. The interpretation tends to claim the person very much as the interpretation "This is a table" is forced upon someone confronted with the sense data. In this it is different from interpretation in the sense of a person organizing data into a meaningful unity by his own efforts.

As man moves away from direct religious experience an ever larger role is assigned to his own interpretations. It is possible, however, for man to arrive at a point where religious experience of any sort disappears. The religious perspective or deeper levels of experience simply no longer suggest themselves. Contemporary man can be said to have come to such a point in his cultural development. Consequently he cannot be expected to move from the secular to a peak or mystical experience directly. Our interest is in keeping open a middle ground, i.e., opening up human experience to the possibility of an authentic religious interpretation.[1]

By the religious dimension of experience or a religious interpretation of experience we mean the viewing of certain experiences of life from the perspective of an ultimate reality beyond. Certain experiences upon reflection and closer examination are recognized as special. They give man pause. They create a sense of awe and mystery. In these man senses an overarching purpose or an ultimate reality. The experiences point beyond themselves. They resist the judgment "that's all there is." Not only do the experiences point beyond, but they point to "a personal more" that is supremely important—the "more" men call God.

---

1. Hopefully, the indirect method, with its emphasis on human experience and its interpretation, will not be confused with religion itself or accepted as a substitute. Religion requires its own special interpretation of experience but is not synonymous with it.

They do not prove God's existence but rather point to him as possible.

A distinction must be made between proving or demonstrating God and pointing to God. The relationship between experience interpreted as pointing to God and the existence of God is not the same as the relationship between an experience of the table and the existence of the table. In the latter case we are outside the order of proof and into the area of direct perception. Unless I assume hallucination, my experience of the table implies the existence of the table. The table is a physical reality without whose actual presence my perception would be impossible. When we talk of God or the divine reality we are not talking about a sensible being with legs and arms, in space and time. God, if he is, is an altogether different sort of reality. A different type of existence requires of necessity a different type of "perception." Where God is concerned, there is no question of verifying, proving, directly experiencing, or even inferring his existence. Some might argue that one or all of the above are possible but it is not our intention here to attempt anything of the sort. Our project is much more modest. It is to look into different human experiences in order to inquire about the possibility of their being interpreted as pointing to God or suggesting the possibility of God.

If one were to hold the nonexistence of God as a dogma, then every human experience which might be interpreted as pointing to God would be automatically judged mistaken. Every instance of direct religious experience (mysticism) would have to be explained away by reducing the alleged experience of God to some other type of experience. On the other hand, to be open to the possibility of certain experiences being interpreted as pointing to God is to move away from dogmatic atheism without going over to a dogmatic theism. Being willing to entertain the possibility of God does not presume the existence of God. If one rejects dogmatic atheism which would settle the question once and for all, experience of any sort notwithstanding, then the possibility of God's existence is presumed. It is this possibility that saves the search for pointers to God from absurdity or leads a person to take seriously the claims of mystics. This, however, is a long way from "proving" the existence of God.

No one experience is guaranteed in every case to open man up to God. For some it might be an experience of the birth of one's own child; for another an experience of the death of a loved one; for still another some event or relationship in between. At these "special times" the question of the purpose of life or the source of being is posed with particular force. These experiences suggest the possibility of a "more" on whom we depend, and to whom we owe our existence. Existence as it were opens itself onto a deeper level. It poses questions about ultimate ground and ultimate purpose.

One of the unusual aspects of our culture is the fact that it tends to be totally ordinary or completely profane. Life in our culture is filled with special events but it is as though they were specifically designed to prevent the emergence of the religious perspective or a religious interpretation. Our special times are so full of noise and excitement that no opportunity is provided to think or reflect. Our work is filled with life-consuming activity and our relaxation is filled with more activity. All events are ordinary in the sense that they are what they are—nothing more. Critics of our times talk a great deal about banality. The suggestion is made that contemporary man has lost even the capacity for that other kind of experience which potentially at least opens onto the religious dimension. (Maybe we are so fascinated today with collecting antiques because there is nothing about our own ordinary existence worth preserving.) If some ages have invited criticism because their preoccupation with the holy was such that it distracted people from care for the profane, our times might be criticized for the opposite reason. The profane, or the ordinary, makes up the whole of life for us. The holy has been obscured to the point of extinction.

Ordinarily special occasions invite wonder, awe, and reflection upon the deeper significance of the experience. Special events, or persons, usually point beyond themselves and invite further inquiry. They pose questions about ultimate purpose which we have described as religious questions. They do not, however, resolve these questions. The religious dimensions of experience provide occasions for man to discover the meaning of the religious questions. They give him a chance to consider the importance of the "other dimension" of human life. This, however, is a long way from *being religious*. The human experiences which open onto the deeper levels of reality are media through which the religious "object" may be disclosed. Man is a religious animal because the religious dimension of experience is open to him and its interest is more than casual. He is not religious in the sense that he is forced to move in faith toward God. Nor is he religious simply because he asks questions about ultimate purpose.

Faith, Courage, and the Human Psyche

Faith is the connector between a religiously interpreted experience and God. Faith moves man to join with what emerges in his experience as a possibility. On the one hand faith opens up for man a window on the ordinary, permitting him to see in it the "more." On the other hand, it encourages man to reach out toward the "more" which already appears in his experience. God is not an irresistible attraction. Nor is he the object of direct perception. The "perception" of God at best is a call, one which may or may not be answered. As we have already mentioned, the infinite and the absolute approach man through the finite and the relative. No one has seen God. This indirectness makes it necessary for man to take an initiative. If he is neither captured nor overwhelmed he must make an effort to respond. Faith is the name of this important human effort.

It makes no sense to speak about faith in what I have directly present to me. What I believe is different from what I directly perceive. My belief is neither evident nor immediately present to my mind. Faith cannot be confused with something I hold on the basis of direct certitude. And yet there is a cognitive element to faith in the sense that I do *know* what it is I *believe*. As a believer I know the content of my faith. My belief has meaning. It is expressed in cognitive propositions (e.g., Jesus died for our sins). Faith then is a movement of man's will toward God who emerges as a possibility. This movement of faith is associated with knowledge. Some would go farther, and say that faith is rewarded with knowledge.

Those who stress the knowledge associated with faith have to qualify it as nonfactual or highly abstract in character.[1] Faith statements add nothing to purely factual experience (if there is any such thing as purely factual experience). The believer does not "know" something about the world which the nonbeliever ignores. Faith is a movement of the whole person to embrace a reality pointed to by his experience, and in that sense it is accurate to describe it as more existential than intellectual. Rather than knowing more, the religious believer is a person with a new insight or perspective on what is known. He is one who celebrates a new relationship to reality—one characterized by at-one-ment and fundamental meaning. Correspondingly belief creates new life attitudes.

While distinguishing faith from knowledge we have to distinguish it as well from ignorance. If faith is not knowledge in the sense of certitude about factual matters, it is also not ignorance or a commitment to what has absolutely no foundation in fact. Religious belief is not an exercise in absurdity. The ultimate reality toward which a person moves in faith must first be accepted as possible. The analysis of our experience becomes a pointer to that possible ultimate reality. While not certain, God enjoys a degree of probability. Probability is far from direct evidence, but even farther from ignorance or irrationality. The gap between evidence and the reality which appears beyond appearance is bridged by an act of faith. Faith then is always a free act. It is also an act of trust. Making the act of trust can be justified within certain limits. In fact it must be justified, if contemporary man is to move from secular existence to a life of faith.

The justification of faith or explaining the reasons for faith can never dispel the element of doubt in religious faith. Reli-

---

1. Those who refuse to so qualify the knowledge associated with faith are called *gnostics*. Gnosticism was an early Christian heresy and was accorded all the proper rejections. But heresies like old soldiers never die. If they fade away they do so very slowly.

gious faith involves an odd dialectic between certainty and doubt. The existential character of religious faith refers to its involvement of the whole personality. This inwardness or subjective involvement translated into psychological terms means added certainty. Psychologically we are surer about that which requires the commitment of our whole self. But, paradoxically, this commitment and corresponding certitude has to coexist with the objective fact that there may not be an ultimate reality. Our experience might be pointing to a being which *in fact* does not exist. Faith then is never a single act which, once made, is over and finished. Faith involves an element of doubt which is never overcome. Since doubt persists even in lifelong religious practice, faith must be a continuing overcoming. The believer must move again and again to God. Only the closed-minded atheist has no doubts about God.

The certainty-doubt dialectic of faith presents particularly serious problems for contemporary man. Science does not require that he sustain such an uncomfortable split. What science proposes, he either accepts the evidence for or he rejects. In the complaints of modern man about religion one discovers a covert wish that everything were like science. It is, however, not just religion that becomes a matter of complaint but human life itself. Human life requires commitments or choices which cannot be put off till science has offered irrefutable proof. It is as if contemporary man were saying, "How can we be expected to put up with human life or religion under these conditions?" If faith involves continuing overcoming of doubt then it becomes too much to ask. Trusting, when everything is not clear, is difficult enough under any conditions. It becomes exceptionally difficult in an age like our own when everything "real" and "true" is verified by science. There might very well be something wrong with religion and the demands it makes on man. Then again, there might be something wrong with contemporary man who finds it so difficult to believe or to trust. Not everything that exists conforms to scientific standards.

If we were to accept a popular secular caricaturization of religious faith we would have to describe it as a last resort. "When all 'normal' approaches to reality have failed, man resorts to belief." Religious faith in this understanding is the very opposite of science. It is equally opposed to philosophy or any use of reason. Such a caricature makes religious faith either inhuman or infrahuman. The fact is, however, that faith of some sort is part and parcel of every human life, even the most dedicated scientific or philosophic existence. Faith is neither subhuman nor irrational. Faith, rather than being a blindness or an unacceptable irrationality, is actually something which belongs to even the most secular form of human life.

The scientist has *faith* that the persistent application of scientific methodology will bring solutions to problems which up to now have eluded man's best efforts. The most secular man has *faith* that life can be improved by human effort. Frequently he also *believes* in the basic goodness of existence. Every time he makes a purchase he shows a degree of faith in the honesty of the dealer's promise to stand behind his product. The astronauts were surrounded by every conceivable form of sophisticated scientific gadgetry and yet a major element in their courage was the faith they had in the people in Houston who directed the project. Only the most narrow neurotic, or better, only the most autistic person is without faith, and there is general agreement on the necessity of restoring faith for healthy human life.

The question then is not so much whether or not to live by faith. Rather the question is whether or not to live life by religious faith. The various forms of secular faith always involve an element of trust and there is always an assent to something that is believed. In these formal respects, religious faith is not different. The content of religious faith is God or God's graciousness toward man, and this content is formalized in certain "faith statements." Trust permeates religious faith, making it a lived experience and not just an intellectual assent to formulas. What distinguishes religious faith then is not that it involves trust and has content but that the trust and content are qualitatively different. Religious faith is in God, and involves the whole person in a relationship. Man becomes related to God, the source of his being, with both his heart and his mind. For the Christian believer, the relationship to God is even more personalized through the mediation of the person Jesus Christ.

The similarities between religious faith and forms of secular belief are in some sense more impressive than the differences between them. As we have seen, every human life involves faith in *something* (not proven by scientific method). At the heart of human reality is a view of reality, a perspective, a *Weltanschauung*. Nietzsche, the father of atheism, has shown that reality for the human being cannot be intellectually analyzed and verified down to its roots but rather requires belief. Nietzsche *believed* that God was dead. Furthermore the faith which stands at the roots of life involves some sort of trust or commitment. A person orders his or her life in terms of what is believed. Nietzsche made his life a testimony to his atheistic faith. He trusted, committed himself, literally lived his faith to the death.

We often hear that the crucial battle in contemporary life is between belief and unbelief. It would be more accurate to say that the battle is not between those who have faith and those who are without it but rather between those who have different faiths. Everyone has faith. Consider all the faith that is required to accept a Marxist interpretation of life and history. The scientists must believe in a certain overall paradigm in which he carries out his particular research. We could enumerate all the traditional forms of philosophical faith. Today many new and oftentimes bizarre faiths have arisen. People today are believers in astrology, devil worship, magic, etc. On the street we see followers of Eastern faiths and Indian faiths. New forms of psychotherapy have attracted believers who practice them "religiously." Each faith has its own specific content, and commitments associated with it give rise to many radically different life styles.

The Marxist believes that economics is the basic reality and that a socialist Utopia is coming in the near or distant future. Correspondingly he trusts and commits himself to this proposal. The positivistic scientist considers Marxism an unverifiable myth, but he in turn believes in the truth of a certain paradigm within which he operates and to the substantiation of which he dedicates his life in research. His style of life will be very different from that of the Marxist. A third person might consider both the above "faiths" untenable and believe rather in the radical absurdity of all reality, the human person included. Following from this belief could be nihilistic anarchism or a dedication to humanism *à la* Camus. A Nazi believes in Aryan supremacy and commits himself to the extermination of Jews. A person today might disbelieve in all the above. He might believe only in himself. "What's good for me is good." Associated with what could be called "naive individualism" might be a belief in free enterprise, America, male superiority, or whatever. The style of life associated with this last "faith" is one that we know too well to waste time describing. The point is that there are many faith contents and just as many different faith commitments with their corresponding life styles.

Associated with every faith there will be an appeal to some event in the past that is presumed to have a special significance. We might say that every faith creates its own history or appropriates its own specific past. People believe this or that because something happened in the past which has central and crucial significance. For the Marxist it might be the writing of *Das Kapital* or the beginning of the Russian Revolution. For the scientist it might be the date of a certain experiment or the publication of its findings. The anarchist will hold certain past events to be important or celebrate the birthday of a famous cobeliever. For the naive individualist everything begins with his appearance on the scene and with other "important" dates associated with himself (e.g., "the day I got my doctorate," or "the day I made vice president," or "the day I reached $1 million in liquid assets"). A Jewish believer will hold the Exodus-Covenant experience of his ancestors to be central. The superpatriot might look at everything in light of the American Revolution. A Christian will point everything to the life and death of Christ. Religious faith is obviously very difficult for contemporary man but faith belongs to the structure of human existence. The most unreligious of men are most often men of great faith.

While religious faith shares certain generic characteristics with what we have described as secular faith, in its specific aspects it is unique. Religious faith is always a movement beyond oneself and as such it involves risk. Authentic faith is an intimate dialogue with God and such an I-Thou relationship makes important demands upon man. God-relatedness, like every deep and serious relationship, requires a change of heart and mind. The choice of relationship to God entails the choice of a certain style of life which excludes many other possibilities. This choice has serious consequences and can never be made lightly. The person of religious faith is of necessity a person of great courage.

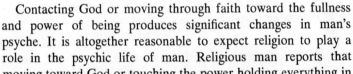

Contacting God or moving through faith toward the fullness and power of being produces significant changes in man's psyche. It is altogether reasonable to expect religion to play a role in the psychic life of man. Religious man reports that moving toward God or touching the power holding everything in existence produces joy, happiness, meaning, identity, a sense of fullness and completeness. Faith which joins the experiencing subject with God, according to the testimony of religious people, produces extraordinary states of consciousness. For articulate expressions of these we rely on the poets and philosophers.

Contemporary secular man might find it easier to relate to the negative testimony. Nietzsche eloquently describes the psychic repercussions of experiencing the death of God. His experience is like that of the great mystics but from the opposite side. He describes the psychic effects of the experience of the absence of God. He speaks of the loss of identity, center, direction, value, hope. He speaks of fear, cold, night, death, guilt. Man for Nietzsche must become God in order to sustain himself in such an experience.

> Whither is god, he cried. I shall tell you. We have killed him—you and I. All of us are his murderers. But how have we done this? How were we able to drink up the sea? Who gave us the sponge to wipe away the entire horizon? What did we do when we unchained this earth from the sun? Whither is it moving now? Whither are we moving now? Away from all suns? Are we not plunging continually? Backward, sideward, forward, in all directions? Is there any up or down left? Are we not

straying as through an infinite nothing? Do we not feel the breath of empty space? Has it not become colder? Is not night and more night coming on all the while? Must not lanterns be lit in the morning? Do we not hear anything yet of the noise of the gravediggers who are burying God? Do we not smell anything yet of God's decomposition? Gods too decompose. God is dead. God remains dead. And we have killed him. How shall we, the murderers of all murderers, comfort ourselves? What was holiest and most powerful of all that the world has yet owned has bled to death under our knives. Who will wipe this blood off us? What water is there for us to clean ourselves? What festivals of atonement, what sacred games shall we have to invent? Is not the greatness of this deed too great for us? Must not we ourselves become gods simply to seem worthy of it?[1]

Hegel articulates the opposite side of the coin. In the following lyrical passage he expresses the positive psychic effects of religion and faith in God.

All that has worth and dignity for man, all wherein he seeks his happiness, his glory, and his pride, finds its ultimate centre in religion, in the thought, the consciousness and the feeling of God. Thus God is the beginning of all things and the end of all things. As all things proceed from this point so all return back to it again. He is the centre which gives life and quickening to all things and which animates and preserves in existence all the various forms of being. In religion man places himself in a relation to this centre in which all other relations concentrate themselves, and in so doing he rises up to the highest level of consciousness and to the region which is free from relation to what is other than itself, to something which is absolutely self-sufficient, the unconditioned, what is free and its own object and end.[2]

Contacting God, if we are to believe the testimony of religious men, is a very positive experience—one which turns

---

1. *The Gay Science* [125], excerpt in W. Kaufmann, *The Portable Nietzsche* (New York: The Viking Press, 1954).
2. G. W. F. Hegel, *Lectures on the Philosophy of Religion*, tr. by E. B. Speirs and J. Burdon Sanderson (London: Kegan Paul, 1962), p. 2.

human life around (*conversion* from the Latin *vertor, verti, versus*—to turn). A new dignity and worth emerge along with personal integration and identity. *Salvation* is a word some have used to describe this many-faceted existence. Hope is one of its important ingredients. Optimism replaces depression or despair because no matter what the present appearances, ultimately there is goodness. The power of being offers promise. God becomes the source of courage to affirm oneself in the face of nonbeing. If the core and center of reality is not against us but with us, there is never final tragedy.

Chapter 10

Finding God in
Human Experience

Admitting that the God experiences reported by religious people have been very positive and that the experiences of the death of God or absence of God have been terrifyingly negative, the God problem is not thereby solved. What is psychically satisfying does not necessarily exist. After all the testimony from religious people about the role of God in their lives, the question remains—Can I believe? Is there any way of relating God's existence to my own life?

What personal experiences can serve as material for religious reflection? What are the privileged areas of human existence which invite reflection on the possibility of God? Are there in the unique dimensions of human existence signs of a "something more"? Are some experiences simply deeper and more meaningful, such that they actually invite a religious interpretation? Is there anything in man's experience of himself as a physical being in space and time that might be religiously significant? Is there, for example, in life experienced as contingent or nonnecessary, a pointer to the ground or foundation of life? Are there in the experiences of the radical limitations of existence (death, suffering, guilt, anxiety, meaninglessness, despair, loneliness) pointers to what is beyond the limit—beyond death, perfect, full of meaning? Can the existence of God be shown to be believable through an analysis of various aspects of my own experience?

Death and God

Salvation is a structural element of religion and therefore found in all major religious traditions. In Hinduism salvation is deliverance from temporal existence. It is the attainment of knowledge and insight that leads to the ultimate and true form of existence, which is eternal. In Buddhism, ethical purification, in the form of extinction of desire, leads to a timeless existence free from suffering. Christianity's doctrine of salvation also involves an overcoming of limitation. Through the proper use of his freedom, man can bring himself to Christlikeness which in turn will make him a sharer of Christ's inheritance—eternal life. ("This day you will be with me in Paradise.") In Christianity man can use his freedom to deny God—thereby remaining a purely natural being for whom death is the end. Or he can use his freedom to move into a relationship with God that brings man God's very life. God's life which is eternal life saves man from the finality of physical death. "Saving one's soul" or bringing oneself to fulfillment in Christianity or in other religious forms is a conquest of space and time in the form of one's own immortality.

Man's religiousness, then, understood as a desire for salvation, is related to the experience of his own physical or biological existence. Besides having a capacity for reflective thought, the human person has a strong biological drive to live. We can describe man as having an instinct for life or an instinct for survival. A reflective analysis of human experience shows up an awareness on the part of each person of his own individuality. It also manifests a desire to preserve individuality, a desire to persevere. There is in man a hunger for life that cannot be satisfied with the prosaic banalities of everyday existence. Everyday existence witnesses to its own inadequacy. There is a gnawing sense of insufficiency that remains just below the surface of our daily rounds which upon reflection surfaces as a demand for *full* life. There is in every man who lives deeply a rebelliousness against superficiality, against lesser forms of life, and ultimately against death. Man's will to life or instinct for survival is not limited by sixty or seventy years but rather is a will *never to pass completely from existence*. Human beings in every age and every culture have pursued salvation, understood as some form of overcoming the physical limitations of life.

In the struggle for survival that is the core of animal life, we can find a symbol of life that survives death. In the unendingness of love as lived by great lovers we can glimpse a human attitude that is not extinguished in death. In the vanity that infects this world and all that passes away we can perceive the other pole, a life that is substantial rather than vacuous and that does not pass away. Is there not, in man's thirst always for more in life, a suggestion that he might be thirsting for a being without limits? The pursuit of love that does not fade points to life which escapes corruption. Does the preoccupation with death characteristic of human beings not show man to be that creature for whom eternal death is abhorrent? It is the experience of death and a shrinking from total annihilation that founds man's hope for salvation in some form of eternal life.[1]

There is no denying that our reason finds even the possibility of continuing existence unacceptable. That which exists for scientific reasoning is that which can be measured, verified, controlled, and predicted. God and the possibility of continued life cannot meet these standards. The man formed in our culture's rationality is advised to face "the facts" and by "the facts" is meant that which science establishes. "The fact" is that death is final. There is "no sense" resisting the inevitable. The longing for a "more," or for life that does not utterly cease, in the context of contemporary rationality, has to be termed a sickness. But who are the sick and who are the healthy? Is scientific

---

1. Perhaps the doctrine of hell, so repulsive to contemporary sensitivities, is nothing more than the frustration of man's drive for survival. Hell is a return to nothingness. The intolerance in certain people for even the suggestion of such a possibility as hell may be a form of resentment against complete annihilation.

reasoning man's only form of intelligence? Can a sick culture set itself up as a standard for health?[1] There are many things which certainly would be judged unreasonable were it not that we have grown accustomed to them. It is "unreasonable" that a small seed should make a great tree or that there should be billions of universes. Perhaps it is only weakness and not reason which induces contemporary man to substitute "making a mark in society" for a real, personal immortality.

People may not talk about salvation in polite society, and yet there remains a preoccupation with some form of immortality. Vance Packard showed just how strong this "modern" version of the instinct for survival really is. The struggle for status is one contemporary form of the instinct. People pursue status today as the medieval man pursued indulgences and with the same overtones of exaggeration. Status means to make a name, to stand out, to be noticed. It drives us and our neighbors to frenzied activity. No sacrifice is too great for its attainment. Notice, for example, the extent to which a contemporary artist like Andy Warhol will go "to be different"—"to stand out," to be "original." The artist seems ready to be a public fool if only he is noticed. Even talent and truth are sacrificed for "glory" or "a place in history"! The artist, in a sense, however, is everyman. The more he is unique, or eccentric, the more immortal he is by secular standards.

Struggling for status makes contemporary society a place of great tension. The saint sacrificed for eternal life. He would preserve his memory in God. Modern man runs the race for a more perishable crown. He would be remembered by his fellows. The tragedy is, few are remembered and they not for long.

In the experience of those who live intensely there is little concern with status, but there is a sense of reality which survives death. Plato, Spinoza, Kant, some of the greatest philoso-

---

1. Faith is a form of sickness according to Freud, but the doubt lingers about Freud's health and the sanity of his ideas on religion. Some recent biographers have gone so far as to suggest the supreme heresy—Freud was sick.

phers, understand human existence as pointing beyond biological existence toward eternal life. Continuing life is held up as
the very heart of human existence. Immortality, for them, is a
possibility rooted in man's very nature. If this is so, God
emerges as the ground of man's continuing existence. God is
pointed to in such experience as the only possible guarantee that
memory, which links me to a past which is no longer, will
persist into a future that is not yet.

Socrates might be taken as giving interesting testimony to
such an experience. In Plato's *Symposium* Socrates explains
that every human creature is a drive for eternity and immortality. Physical love, for him, is part of every authentic life because
love is a creative or procreative drive. The force of sexual love
for him is explained as a desire on the part of mortal nature for
immortality. A person lives on "in a sense" in the other whom
he procreates. The universal phenomenon of human love then is
for Socrates "an interest for the sake of immortality." "Think
only of the ambition of men, and you will wonder at the sense-
lessness of their ways unless you consider how they are stirred
by the love of an immortality of fame. Nay . . . I am persuaded
that all men do all things, and the better they are, the more they
do them, in hope of the glorious fame of immortal virtue; for
they desire the immortal."[1]

Socrates not only saw in his analysis of human experience a
desire for immortality but later (in the *Apology*) reasoned to
the actual immortality of man's spirit. Socrates faced his own
death with a confidence that he was not passing away totally.
What he found in man's emotional life—his passions, his instincts, his sexual drives—he uses as intellectual support in his
arguments for the soul's immortality. All this suggests a question about the nature of human experience. Was Socrates de-
luded into thinking that man desires immortality? Is it the case
that human nature as we experience it in our time has lost its
fire or its depth or perhaps its guts? Does human life lived
deeply really point beyond itself, or is this nothing more than a

---

1. Plato, "Symposium," *The Dialogues of Plato*, 3rd ed., trans. Benjamin
Jowett (New York & London: Oxford University Press, 1892), 1:577.

pious wish? Does the demand of realism require that we abandon such hope or is there reason for hope built into the very reality of human existence? Are the philosophers we mentioned dreamers or human beings with a deeper grasp of human being? If man is immortal, then God—the guarantee of a yet fuller existence—is pointed to by life itself.

Man's appetite for life is a desire to go on, or a repulsion at the thought of utterly ceasing to be. Each of us has the experience of wanting to change. There is no one who would not like to be like someone else in this or that way (for example, looks, weight, intelligence). There is no one, however, who wants *to be* the other person. We want to be ourselves, with this or that change worked into the context of our life. Becoming the other person would mean ceasing to be. This we resist. The man of flesh and blood wants to be. The human being can do more that think about eternal life, as an intellectual possibility. He can feel and desire it in the very marrow of his bones. Such a deeply felt experience, while certainly not proving God's existence, might be interpreted as pointing to God.

The God pointed to in a reflective analysis of man's will to live or his deep desire for a fullness of life is not the God of reason or rational argument. Reason, at least as we use it today (scientific reason), seems rather to require "knuckling under" to the fact of death and its appearance of finality. God, who corresponds to man's will to live or desire not to cease utterly, is a God of hope. If man is just as truly will or desire as he is reason or intellect, then there seems nothing incongruous in talk of a God of hope. (The man who is nothing but reason or pure intelligence is obviously lacking.)

A strong desire of this sort might seem very strange to contemporary secular man, accustomed as he is to planned obsolescence. When things become paradigms even for human existence, then it seems "only reasonable" that life too be "disposed of" once its usefulness has ceased. We throw away empty bottles, don't we? Wanting to go on living seems both irrational and unrealistic. It is, however, possible that contemporary man's idea of what is realistic or reasonable is actually less than real or rational. It might be possible that contemporary man has lost the sense of deeply lived human existence. The apathy we spoke of in Part 1 may be at the root of contemporary man's problem with religion. We know there are many emotionally ill people today who suffer from a loss of feeling. We know too that so-called normal people can be deficient in feeling. Are today's psychiatric patients reflective of a disease affecting our whole culture? Are we suffering from "affective stupidity"? Have we forgotten how to really cry and really laugh, or to love or to touch the deeper levels of our lives?

Facing death courageously, which we discussed in Part 2 of the book, has nothing to do with giving in to the fact of death or giving up hope for an even fuller life. In fact, for Socrates belief and hope in immortality were the key to his courage. It is one thing to have to die. The question is, does death mean to die utterly—to cease being? The God possibility hinges on a proper interpretation of lived experience. Is human life an accident finally to be hauled to the dump, or does human life manifest an intention and a purpose which spills over the very boundary of death?

Let's suppose for a moment that the answer is negative. Human life has no purpose, and it witnesses to no intention. My personality is an accident in a world of accident and chaos which has no enduring future. As a person I will soon be nothing. My consciousness will become complete unconsciousness. My accomplishments, my insights will all come to nothing and so it will be with all the rest. Plato and Einstein share a common fate with the worst idiot. No one will survive. My fate without immortality is the fate of the whole species. Man's concern with salvation in this case is either an absurd exercise or an effort which witnesses to the unacceptability of such a fate. Is despair an ingredient of my senseless existence or is it possible that despair is not final? Is the desire not to die a pointer to the possibility that life is "something more" than it appears? Is the *felt* unacceptability of despairing existence itself a pointer to the possibility of hope for life?

The testimony of Socrates and other philosophers requires that we look critically at the nature of our experience. There is no question about our being able to get along as we are. Man can get along without deep feeling, and without critical reflection, just as he can get along without good eyesight or any sight at all. The question concerns the quality of our existence. We must wonder whether our scientifically founded culture has not led us into an affective deprivation. Have we today lost a deep feeling for individual life and the strong desire for survival? According to Spinoza, a strong feeling for life, a desire to persist and not to die completely constitutes the very essence of human life. If this is so then the very essence of man points to the possibility of God who makes fullness of life possible.

Starting from the same physical level of human experience, a very different approach to the possibility of God might be taken. The same spatio-temporal condition which founds man's struggle with death also constitutes the possibility of science. Science addresses itself to spatio-temporal reality rather than a world of ideals or pure forms. Because it is man who uses the methodologies and instruments of science, science is a human endeavor. We talked about science above in terms of its influence on the creation of contemporary culture and secular man. Its development and application to technology created the conditions for the evolution from medieval religious society toward contemporary secular society. Science then can be said to have been the most influential force behind the first culture in the history of man without a God experience. Oddly enough, however, the same science has been seen by some to be the road back to religion. The experience of science can be one of those privileged experiences which upon reflection actually point to the possibility of God. How?

Science most recently has moved beyond an analysis of our small planet into the larger universe. It has become cosmic or interspatial or interstellar. Turning its attention to this broader horizon has given all of us a new experience of the universe. New and astounding vistas of space and time have been presented. These in turn tend to create a sense of awe. The universe which science reveals is beyond man's powers of comprehension or even objectification. Mystery has returned to secular man's experience via the very instrument and methodologies which originally presumed to eliminate mystery. The early scientists thought they had a line on each of the bodies in space and could track its movements and direction. Today, the universe appears to be so immense that it defies the most abstract explanations of its parts and their interrelationships. Through science turned toward space, we are treated to an experience very close to that of the desert dweller in Biblical times who without lights or smog to dim the display looked up to the sky, i.e., the experience of reality that overwhelms, that is beyond man, that is mysterious and awe-inspiring. This experience does not prove the existence of God but it is one which might point to God. Experiencing awe and mystery, or catching a glimpse into reality that transcends us, is not necessarily religious experience but it is very close to religion.

Because man's powers of reflection are what they are, they make possible an unlimited number of perspectives on a reality as complex as human life. One after another aspect of the same human experience might provide the material for reflection from the perspective of God or religion. Let's try one more way of viewing man as a physical being.

Being physical means being nonnecessary or contingent. Man's being does not include necessity. The fact that the universe exists does not reveal the necessity of its existence or its endurance in existence and the same is true of man. Man happens to be, but tomorrow he might not be. Surrounding man's being and the being of everything else in the universe is an abyss of nonbeing.

You, my reader, are where you are, but not by any necessity, and consequently there is a void surrounding your being. At any moment the void might move in. The longer you live, the more you accomplish, the greater the sense of your life's precariousness. At any moment it could all be gone.

The void surrounding human life is experienced as a threat. It is the same void which surrounds all existing reality, even the cosmos, and yet that fact offers little consolation. To offset the anxiety created by this situation man presumes that "things will go on as usual," but this presumption is always being interrupted by the *un*usual. These interruptions increase man's uneasiness. The anxiety and uneasiness might dispose one person to escape in noise and activity but for another they might be a reason for pause. The radical contingency of human life suggests a question about the nature of reality.

Is reality ringed by a void and that's all? Or does contingency point to its opposite: the necessary? Ultimately is there just a void? Or ultimately is there a reality that is responsible for both being and the void? Does the very existence of the void point to what is required for there to be void—i.e., being? Does the void point beyond itself to what is necessary for its existence, i.e., being that is not rimmed by nonbeing? What is the ultimate reality: the void, nonbeing, nothingness? Or is the ultimate reality just the opposite: the fullness of being, eternal being, God? The experience of contingency might be interpreted as final and the reason for nonbelieving. The experience brings man, however, if reflected upon, to the point where he has either to assert that the void is ultimate or seriously to consider the possibility of the opposite proposition, i.e., that God is and he is ultimate.

Intelligence and God

Man experiences himself as something more than just a physical being. He is also spiritual, i.e., a being who thinks, is aware, has insights, and engages in reflection. None of these functions can be reduced to his physical or biological existence. They do not follow the laws governing physical things. Besides the drive for survival which we talked about in association with man's biology, human experience includes also a drive to understand. Human beings inquire and pursue meaning. They strive to fit fundamental meanings into coherent systems which claim to *make sense* of existence. To flee from understanding is to flee from humanness. Seeking truth is as important to man as seeking security.

The relationships between inquiring and humanness were explored above in Part 2 of the book. Here we return to this aspect of human existence to ask whether in the analysis of man's spirituality we can find a pointer to God. Here again we are attempting to found an inquiry into the possibility of God upon an analysis of the human condition. Our task is not to look outside man, to the nature and function of objects in the world but rather to look within man, to the experience of the human person. For this approach to work the reader must do more than read. He must allow the experience described to take place within himself. We saw how the experience of limit or death must be existentially entertained, i.e., experienced in concrete individual terms within one's own life. The same is so of the experience of inquiry. First man must exercise his spirituality. He must become an inquirer. Then we can begin to search this experience for signs or pointers to God.

In some cases the experience of inquiry is missed because it takes place so seldom. Most frequently it is involved with something outside man and rarely turns back on inquiry itself. The experience of inquiring or questioning awareness is, however, both unique to man and very complex. I am asked a difficult question. The problem presents itself not in the context of natural environment but through the medium of symbols (nonphysical realities). I *understand* the question. "I grasp" the problem. Then I begin to recollect events, sort out relevant data, formulate a response that is coherent and intelligible both to the questioner and to myself. Finally I organize this response into sounds which communicate meaning. In some case I might at the same time be aware that it is I who am conscious and inquiring, and that my self-awareness is different from the other acts of reasoning.

The uniqueness of these experiences separates man from all other *things* or objects or animals, and consequently different language and different methods of explanation are required for understanding man. Because of intelligence, awareness, reflective consciousness, we cannot do justice to man by using language derived from objects, or physical laws, or even Skinner's pigeons. John Updike uses literature rather than philosophy to express the point of man's difference. "It seemed to me from this sunset hour that the world is our bride, given us to love, and the terror and joy of marriage is that we bring to it a nature not our bride's."[1] *Spirituality* is one way of describing the functions which separate man from the purely *physical*.

In less literary language, we could say that man experiences his consciousness as very different from the objects of the world with which it is most frequently engaged. Even the generally unreflective person who is almost exclusively preoccupied with "the outside" (job, car, weather, house, etc.) is forced in privileged moments to recognize if only dimly that as a conscious being he lives in two worlds that do not always coincide. His thoughts, his questions, a moment of insight or reflection are not the same as the starlit night which might have set all these in motion. The outside world of objects is over against his consciousness. If he lives exclusively in the former he becomes thingified. If he lives exclusively in the latter he abides in the private world of thought. Perhaps only dimly, but human beings do realize that their conscious awareness sets them apart. Some call this nonobjective experience the spiritual life, to distinguish it from the physical world outside.

Man is called an inquiring spirit because he never ceases to question the reality he confronts. Sometimes the questioning is explicit and he searches to understand what things are in themselves, independently of their relationship to his life (the sciences). In other cases it takes the form of an intelligent interest in what goes on about him and affects his life (the humanities). Not all men are equally inquisitive but all strive for some degree of understanding. In some cases there is a hesitancy and reserve about inquiry and understanding because these might threaten comfort, convenience, security, but such behavior smacks of neurosis. We admire the inquiring man and we value understanding. The Greek emphasis on intelligence as the key to humanness is still an attractive thesis. To call a man stupid is a debasing insult because to be intellectually alert, and to understand, is what we expect of human beings.

---

1. *Pigeon Feathers* (New York: Alfred A. Knopf, 1962), pp. 277, 278.

Many different phrases and metaphors have been devised to describe the peculiar experience of understanding. It is frequently compared to the sense of sight, and talked of as seeing or perceiving. Objects and organs too are used to describe it. Understanding is spoken of as "getting the *point*," "*grasping* the *material*," "detecting the *pattern*," "coming to the *heart* of the matter." It is difficult to find appropriate language to describe this experience for the simple reason that our language is richer in object words. We live in a world of objects and constantly employ our senses. We have more words for objects and sense functions. But human experience is not exhausted by these. We do also understand. We know what we mean by the phrase "getting the point." The appetite of inquiry is nourished by acts of understanding. Man is a questioning animal and understanding is the reward of his inquiry.

Understanding, however, is never the end of inquiry. It is never final. Man's appetite is never satiated. Every act of understanding, because it is not complete, suggests still another question. Every achievement opens up another line of inquiry. In practical matters a person decides that such an understanding or bit of knowledge is enough and does not pursue a question further. But the possibility of continuing inquiry is shut off by a decision of the subject and not by any objective completeness. As a matter of fact, what is accepted today as understood will sometime later likely require further inquiry because the previous "insight" or "knowledge" will become inadequate. All human beings search after understanding, test insights, reflect, and build their meanings into coherent systems ("philosophy"). Man wants to know, and the whole of reality is the opposite pole of this desire. Faithfulness to understanding is one of the important conditions for community. Human beings everywhere are people in dialogue—i.e., exchanging insights, inquiring, reflecting, experiencing, understanding. Meanings make man. Shared meanings make society.

What does this experience have to do with God? Is there anything in the experience that might point to the possibility of God? Can we justify taking a religious perspective on this experience? One way to answer these questions is in the negative.

For some contemporary atheists it is precisely man's drive to understand which founds the absurdity of human life (Camus). Man is a relentless drive to understand, and there is nothing to which this drive corresponds. The world is chaos because there is no creator who ordered all things. There are no meanings to satiate man's appetite. He is then an absurd animal—a drive for what is nonexistent. His lot is one of frustration and despair. Human beings appeared amid the chaos by a cruel stroke of black fate. They are caught in a web of contradictions. Man is bounced back and forth in ping-pong fashion between contradictory poles of existence; the drive for meaning and the absence of meaning. Only death relieves this useless tragedy.

A reflective analysis of man's spirituality then certainly cannot be said to prove the existence of God. Can it, however, be looked at differently or interpreted otherwise than from the atheist view? Does the very articulation of the atheistic interpretation suggest a possibility of an alternative perspective? Is it not possible to see in man's questioning and drive to understanding not absurdity but meaning? Reality shows itself amenable to questioning, and research is rewarded by understanding. The world reveals itself to us as structured, and able to be understood. There is a complementarity between man's questioning and "reasons" that are available. Given this situation, man's relentless questioning can be interpreted not as absurd but rather as manifesting purpose or intention. One might inquire about the source of both man's spirit and the correlative meaningful reality. One single creative source of both man and the world is at least suggested by their complementarity. God emerges as the possible source of both. The relentless drive that stands behind every question and the consciousness which realizes the unfinished character of every answer suggest intelligence as a constituent human element. An analysis of experiences of understanding at the very least suggests the opposite of absurdity. It gives an intimation of order, purpose, and intention. In the drive to understand which precedes every inquiry, as well as in the understanding which crowns its success, we catch a glimmer of God who himself is supreme understanding and the source of inquiry and insight.

Even the thoroughly secular man prides himself in being a thinker. His success in business or industry or science depends upon his inquiring mind. It is persistence in pursuing difficult solutions which marks the successful secular man. In his life then there is the experience of intelligent awareness as well as the experience of insight and understanding. The world in which he operates he has shown time and again to be open to analysis. His business charts and plans are presumed to be a reflection of the way things are. Our interest here is to open this whole experience to a reflection from the perspective of religion. Is the experience of inquiry and understanding an accident? Does it show up a fundamentally absurd reality? Or rather the opposite? Does understanding as an experience as well as the drive for understanding suggest the possibility of an intelligent source?

The God suggested by this reflection is not the God of will or desire we talked about in the preceding section. He is the spirit of intelligence which makes reality intelligible and makes it possible for man to understand. God is not the answer to my questions, or the missing link in my philosophical system. God so conceived is prior to systems or preferred philosophies. He makes systems and philosophies possible. God is the source of man's questioning and the source of the intelligibility man finds in reality. Neither of these experiences seem to point to man's situation as one of chaos or absurdity. The experiences certainly do not prove God. They are admittedly less than overwhelming and for some will be too abstract to be convincing. For others, however, the experience of intelligent inquiry points beyond itself. The existence of explanations points to a reason why there are explanations; the appetite for understanding points to a source of such a mysterious drive. Without God, the whole world of inquiry and penetrating understanding is arbitrary and fortuitous.

The God whose possibility we are considering is certainly not the God of most faithful churchgoers. I do not mean to "knock the person in the pew." (That's a game played by too many superficial "intellectuals" to be in any way attractive.) Saying that many "ordinary" believers do not relate to the God we have been trying to suggest is not meant as a put-down. Many people believe by conditioning, complacency, and convention; others by passion, emotion, desire, hope. The least part of "ordinary" belief is that played by the critical intelligence, which we are claiming points to God. The situation is not very different for the "ordinary" unbeliever. He disbelieves most often because of different conditioning, complacency, and convention. The unbeliever most frequently denies the God of critical intelligence by refusing ever to entertain a religious perspective. He shuts the God of intelligence out just as definitively as does the "ordinary" believer. Critical intelligence in the form of persistent questioning is rare in both camps. God is dead for many an atheist because serious consideration of God is deliberately rejected. Turning to God in the sense we have been describing him would require a conversion on the part of believer and unbeliever alike.

To speak of the experience of man's spirituality as possibly pointing to God must not be taken to mean pointing to a cosmic order of classical design. Reality might present itself to man as meaningful without being perfectly ordered. Man's drive for understanding joins with a correlative reality but not perfect rational order. Reality is intelligible but its intelligibility includes an awareness of the irrational, upsets, surds, and catastrophes. The suggestion of God from an analysis of man's spirituality is not a suggestion that reality is perfectly intelligible. Belief in God does not include belief in a perfectly ordered universe. The unexpected or the unintelligible is also part of human experience. God is intimated in the human experiences of inquiry or understanding and these need not—indeed cannot—ever be perfect.

Inquiry and understanding are not out of harmony with the universe despite its imperfections. Moreover these experiences seem not to be accidental but rather purposeful—yielding a clue to the riddle of human existence. It seems incredible that human nature and the whole of reality could be absurd. If everything is absurd then nothing is absurd. Rather it seems that the human condition in the sense of man's spirituality pursues and finds some intelligible pattern everywhere. Persistent intelligent inquiry turns up *explanations* where before none seemed to exist. Freud, for example, saw patterns of purpose even in the most psychotic behavior. Explanations differ, develop, are replaced by other explanations, but in all of this, inquiry and understanding are constant. If reality is absurd and man a tragic accident, the very apex of stupidity would be the university (an institution dedicated to the pursuit of what is not) or any human institution valuing intelligence. If, on the other hand, the drive for understanding is in harmony with a reality that is intelligible then at least we can entertain the possibility of God as the source of both.

In summary, then, this reflection proceeds from the experience of intelligence to the suggestion of God as its source. Intelligence in our reflections has a subjective and an objective pole. It refers to the drive for understanding in man which is not exhausted either by the "common sense" meanings of a culture or by the most sophisticated scientific explorations. The subjective appetite moreover is in harmony with a world which bares its reasons to persistent inquiry. We experience a congruence between man's drive for understanding and an objective reality that lends itself to understanding. Man suffers all sorts of alienation and estrangement, evils and absurdities, but he also experiences the beautiful, the good, the intelligible. Man is an inquirer, *at home* in any intelligible world. But how can we justify such an experience without God who is the source of both man's inquiring spirit and intelligible reality? How could this twofold intelligibility be an unintelligible freak or an absurd chaotic accident? It seems implausible that man's intelligence *just happens* to be in harmony with an intelligible reality which also *just happened*.

This particular perspective on man's experience must not be taken to claim too much. Our suggestion is actually very modest. Calling attention to the experience of understanding does not claim that our understanding is final. It makes no pretense of *actually* achieving terminal insight. Perhaps the myths of the "primitives" are as sophisticated and as plausible as the contemporary "myths" of science. Complete and final understanding of ourselves or the world is always out of reach. Our emphasis is not on the achievements of intelligence but on the experienced fruitfulness of continuing inquiry. Little by little, and not necessarily in a straight-line type of progressive evolution, inquiry corrects earlier understanding. Understanding takes place because of the harmony between man's capacities and the world in which he exists. Is man's unique intellectual restlessness, which both leads to understanding and shows up the limits of every intellectual advance, absurd? Is man's inquiring spirit which always asks another question a drive ultimately toward nothing? Or rather does it point both to a source and to a fulfillment in God who made man an inquirer, and is himself man's final goal? "Our hearts were made for Thee, Oh Lord, and they shall not rest until they rest in Thee."

The experiences we are considering from a religious perspective do not exhaust human experience. If reflection upon intelligence draws man toward the possibility of God there are other experiences that seem to draw him in the opposite direction. Children starve, droughts and floods ravish human life, man who understands and longs for immortality is killed in absurd accidents. Institutionalized religion is a community of sinners. Unjust social orders grind away at the poor and the unpowerful. These experiences draw man toward unbelief. But reflection upon man's being, his peculiar human experience, draws him in the opposite direction. There is no way to prove one conclusion over another. The God question is linked to differing interpretations of human experience. Its resolution depends upon what *we choose* to emphasize in our experience. Being faithful to the experience of inquiry and understanding in the sense of facing up to the implications of such an experience does, however, point strongly toward God who makes insight possible.

Evil and God

No God talk can hope to be convincing unless it makes an honest effort to grapple with the most powerful arguments against God, all of which come from the many-faceted reality of evil. The arguments used by apostolic atheists are basically the same ones which the believer has to cope with in order to sustain honest belief. The many different forms of the argument can be subsumed under the following formula. "A normally good person would do all he could to prevent evil. If God exists and is good then he should do likewise. But there is evidence everywhere that evil exists. God does not prevent it. How can God be, and be good, and be almighty, and yet permit the evil which plagues human existence? Therefore, God does not exist."

Philosophers would find all sorts of problems with this generic argument. One might call attention to the fact that all the key terms in the argument (good, person, almighty) are applied to God in the same sense that we use them for human beings. Another would object to judging God by the standard of a "good, middle-class, English gentleman." Still others might insist that the argument is founded upon an unsophisticated, naive, fundamentalist conception of omnipotence—which presumes God to be a kind of genteel superman in the sky. All these objections are well founded but they are beside the point. It is a fact that the ordinary people who must wrestle with the God problem are not professional philosophers. Professional subtleties escape them. People have to use some model for organizing and understanding reality and the God reality is no exception. The most commonly used model in the case of God is that of a "good man." God is thought of as a gentleman. As such he is open to the same criticisms any gentleman would receive for his behavior. The very idea of a transcendent God, beyond praise and blame, is at best extremely difficult for people to comprehend. The God whom people are introduced to in catechism, Sunday School, or bar mitzvah instruction is one who makes moral laws, prescribes justice, and punishes sin (a moral agent). It is therefore understandable that people tend to judge God by some type of moral standard.

The existence of evil then is *the* problem for a believer and *the* foundation for every atheistic faith. Belief, whether it involves an affirmation of God, or a rejection of God, in order to be rational must be supported by intelligent and critical reasoning. The believer then *and* the unbeliever must "reason together" about the problem of evil. They both experience physical evil: they both suffer pain; they both know about drought, starvation, disease, earthquakes, cancer, etc. This evidence the unbeliever uses to reason to God's nonexistence. "No good God could permit such things to happen." Such happenings not only violate "good order" but even more do they stand in opposition to the image of an "all-powerful middle-class gentleman." The believer is hard pressed by the same evil but hesitates to make the atheistic "act of faith." He is reminded of the insistence in Biblical literature that God not be judged by human standards, or by strictly human concepts of value and order. "His ways are not our ways." Then, too, the God who is revealed in Scripture is not the middle-class gentleman with superman powers. Neither is he the eighteenth-century superarchitect, who supposedly manufactured a world of marvelous order and symmetry. Rather he is a God of mystery and paradox. He is a God who time and time again works in strange ways. He is Job's God, held to and trusted despite every conceivable type of evil. The believer, then, troubled as he is by the experience of evil, holds on to his beliefs on the assumption that God works in mysterious ways, or that God's will is unfathomable and yet just. Besides these "faith" supports for belief in God we have been suggesting that reason too can support belief. A reasoned analysis even of negative experiences can point beyond themselves to God. We continue in this vein by suggesting that an analysis of the experience of evil in the sense of moral evil or sin can have religious significance.

The God whose possibility we have already suggested is not at variance with the Biblical image of God (*Yahweh*). Human experience of space and time points to a Biblical God of hope rather than the middle-class gentleman type of deity. It was evil in the sense of negative elements or painful limitations imposed by space and time (sickness and death) from which we moved to the possibility of God. Job's God is such a God of hope. The experience of intelligence also suggests something other than the eighteenth-century god of perfect order. The drive to understand recognizes the irrational, the surd, disorder, and unintelligibility. It points to a God who is the source of these evils as well as of the intelligible structures of reality. Nowhere in Scripture do we find God as the architect of a logical, perfectly ordered, and altogether good reality. Scripture portrays God as the author of the intelligible and the absurd—the rational and the idiotic alike. It is not possible to do away completely with the standard images of God as "the good guy upstairs," or "the perfect clockmaker," but these images at least can be shown to be narrowly cultural, unscriptural, and hardly the only standard for judging the God question.

The image of God which comes from attentiveness to Scripture and experience is very different from the powerful gentleman who always intervenes to stop evil. The problem of evil does not go away once we adopt a more intelligent notion of divinity. It continues to challenge religious belief but not in such a distorted way. Reality as we have been considering it includes evil, the evils of suffering, death, meaninglessness, etc. It has been *this real* from which we have attempted to develop our reflections rather than a perfectly ordered reality, where all wrongs are immediately righted by some good superman. The God pointed to by our experience is then the God of a reality which includes evil.

In fact it is the evil-ridden aspects of existence which suggest the possibility of God. Rather than beginning with a world of logic, order, and perfect design which does not exist (and then arguing to the nonexistence of God), we begin with the actual world in which we live our human lives. It is not so much then a question of how a God of order and logic could exist and yet be involved in the disorder in which we live. The God we are pointing to through an analysis of our human experience is linked with the reality we confront daily, which includes imperfection, disorder, the irrational, suffering, and death. Evil continues to be a stumbling block for religion because even with this "more realistic" and more scriptural approach, a question remains: what kind of God does the evil-ridden reality point to? Obviously he is not the "reasonable," domesticated God of our middle-class conventions, but who is he? It is the existence of evil which presses us down and forces us, like Job, to seek out the God in whom we believe. Because this is neither the time nor the place for a full-blown theodicy, we narrow down our consideration of evil in this section to moral evil and begin to probe this experience for pointers to God.

One way to describe moral evil is as a free choice by man against the standards of goodness derived from his very nature. We saw in the section on "Man as Ethical" that man is free and that his freedom is founded on the very structure of his being. Because man is naturally free, he cannot escape the responsibilities of his choices. He must choose, and he must choose either good or evil. He can choose the good in the sense of that which contributes to the fulfillment of human being, or he can choose evil—which mars human existence or diminishes himself and others.

Good and evil are more than words. They are certainly more than expressions of a personal preference, interest, or satisfaction. They are linked to man's essence in that he is structurally a decision maker who has to make his choices on the basis of some standard of good and evil. When man does good, he promotes his being. The definition of good is that which perfects or creates the human. The life of a good person is edifying. Its very presence builds up in those who are associated with the good person a sense of life as basically good and reflective of a good creation. When man does evil, however, the very opposite occurs. Man is capable of dehumanizing himself, misusing his potential, ultimately destroying himself and others. Instinctively man recognizes the inhuman or the dehumanizing as evil. Man can and does do evil, and moral evil like any other mounts a negative witness against God. Those who suffer evil are unedified, torn down, pushed into disbelief in the goodness of life.

In this section we want to reflect on moral evil—with an eye toward seeing that particular experience from a religious perspective. Rather than moving away from God because of immorality we want to suggest that evil in the sense of personal evil or sin is another crucial or central experience from which man may catch a glimpse of God. Sin in other words may provide man with a privileged perspective from which the possibility of God can be seriously entertained.

Karl Menninger in a well-received recent book (*Whatever Became of Sin*) decried the disappearance of sin awareness from our culture. Menninger's perspective is psychiatric and he points up the relationship between sin and mental health. Man's psychic condition cannot be improved while systematically defining out of existence his moral responsibility. Unless man reckons with sin, according to Menninger, he will consistently fail to handle the task of mental health. The disappearance of sin consciousness, then, certainly a fact of modern American culture, is, according to him, not to be applauded. Sin first was redefined as crime and sent to jail. Then it was redefined as psychopathology and sent to a clinic. Gradually sin disappeared from the consciousness altogether. Sin, however, is different from either crime or psychopathology. It cannot be cured by incarceration or removed by any miracle drug. Menninger's point is a simple one. Despite all our cultural redefining, men still commit sin and must face up to this aspect of their lives if they will be whole human beings.

The disappearance of sin has had an effect on more than contemporary man's mental health. It also plays a part in a loss of religious sensitivity or in what we have talked about as the loss of a sense of God. There is a close relationship between the disappearance of moral evil and the development of a culture without a God experience. How are these two experiences linked? What is the connection between an experience of moral failure and an experience of God? In what way can evil (in the sense of moral evil) be seen such that it points to the possibility of God?

To be a man is to be in a situation which demands a created response. Besides being aware of his spatio-temporal limits, or being an animal with a drive for meanings, man is unique also in that his actions are not determined but rather created by himself. Other animals *adjust* to their environment. Man must *create* response to situations and *make them just*. Not only is man required by his nature to create responses to the surrounding outside but he is called to make a response even to his own self. Man's very self is a reality to which he must respond, and his response is creative in the sense that gradually it fashions or creates the responding self. Man makes himself by the way he responds to himself. ("Every day I salute the person I could have chosen to be.") Human existence then is not something "given" and finished but rather a task to be accomplished. Human life is a project (a "something" to be done) which can turn out to be either good or bad.

Contemporary culture has tended to repress this aspect of the human reality. Marxism, for example, tries to convince us that human life can be understood exclusively in terms of a relationship to the world. Human life for Marx is praxis or work or productive involvement with the world. Behaviorists presuppose a similarly defective image. Man for the disciples of Skinner is tied to the outside world so thoroughly that he is nothing more than what the outside dictates. Proper manipulation of the outside will produce any kind of man you like, because man and the outside world are one. Both dominant images, however, leave out the important relationship which man has to himself. The self which each person is, is present to each person, and open to many different types of choice. The outside, work, social relations are important but they do not exhaust the human reality.

Our very selves constitute part of the reality to which we must make an active and creative response. Human beings are turned not only outward but inward. Human consciousness returns upon itself. Because man is related to himself and able to choose himself as this or that person absolutely, he does not dissolve into every passing moment or in every involvement with the outside. The self that is chosen remains itself throughout successive moments of time. Man's self-relatedness makes man *spirit* and not ever reducible to matter or the physical. Self-choice, or spirit, posits in man a real permanence or identity.

According to this perspective man becomes a person through an active concern with his own self (self-relatedness) or following a choice of his own self. Choosing oneself as this or that human being constitutes the human existent as a person. Freedom is of man's very essence and therefore only by exercising freedom in a radical or absolute way does man become himself. Personhood is not given but constituted by a free choice directed to the very self. The human task is one involving the creation of the person I will become, and that creation takes place by the choice I make of a certain self. I become a concrete self only by a concrete choice of the self.

Decision gives definite structure to existence. The person's whole personality is at stake in a life choice. If I choose to marry and raise a family a very different self is created from what I would be if I never so chose but rather just lived for the moment and for pleasure. Because so much is at stake anxiety is always associated with such a decision. The choice is always a risk. There is never only one possibility for a self. The choice of one self is associated with an awareness that the choice might very well not be the best. In addition, one self-choice eliminates many other possibilities. Some persons become immobilized before their many possibilities. Others face the dangers inherent in the human condition and choose but never with equanimity or tranquility. If man is limited but multiple possibility, his condition inevitably involves anxiety which accompanies the critical choices. Even choosing not to choose is a choice and, for the perceptive person who sees the implications of such a move, equally permeated with anxiety. Who can help being anxious about letting life be directed by outside events rather than taking hold of it and managing the outside?

Before definitive self-choice, man is tied to his body. The soul and the body are in close harmony. Pleasure is life's reason for being. The child is the perfect example of the aesthete who lives for the moment and for what is immediately pleasureful. As human beings grow older, however, they *dream of being something*. Man dreams the many possibilities that are there to be actualized by his choice. But as soon as the self posits itself by a definite choice, the body-soul harmony is broken. No longer does body or pleasure lead. The choice constitutes man as an identity and the someone I have chosen to be demands sacrifice. Such a self can no longer live just for pleasure. Values come to be in the definite choice, chosen values, personal values which become more important than pleasure or physical comfort.

The psychological state which precedes this all-important spirit-creating, self-constituting choice is anxiety, perhaps even dread. The aesthetic state is characterized by pleasure and its loss is not taken lightly. To become a self, a "self" must be lost. The determination of existence or the choice of a certain self means the loss of that dreamy state of multiple possibility and immediate pleasure. The anxiety which always accompanies self-choice is an ambivalence that on the one hand wishes to *become someone* and on the other hand dreads *becoming someone*. Some people remain aesthetes and never make the leap because the anxiety is too much to bear. As in every instance of escape, however, the dreadful anxiety ultimately is the victor. If anxiety accompanies the actualization of one of man's many potentialities, despair and an even more painful dread accompany growing old without the continuity of a permanent self or identity. Without the self-determining choice man loses his life in every passing moment. The first anxiety or dread is caused by the abyss which separates the self from all that it might become. The latter dread is caused by the abyss which separates life from what it should have been. "Being able" or freedom is at the root of anxiety.

Not every choice of the self is self-creative. I may choose myself as I am at this moment, in this particular circumstance. In so doing, I choose a relative self, one that is immersed in and characterized by the external circumstance. The self-creating choice is one that chooses a self regardless of the outside conditions, the circumstances, the outside. Traditional marriage is a good example of the absolute choice because it involves an explicit conceptualization of being "beyond the purely external circumstance": "For better or worse, for richer or poorer, in sickness or in health, until death." To choose oneself as so united creates a self that is not relative, or determined by outside circumstance, but precisely the opposite, i.e., a self which transcends the outside condition, even the worst conceivable outside condition.

Marriage is not the only such choice. Any choice of the self which involves a total commitment of the whole of my being, one which endures no matter what, qualifies as self-creating choice. There will be other choices to be made, but this "first" choice or original choice or creative choice endures throughout subsequent choices. (If this original choice is looked upon as a "fall" from the stage of unlimited possibilities into a limited existence, one sees an analogy in individual life to "the original fall" which affects not just every subsequent choice but every subsequent human being.) The choice to go to work as an electrical appliance repairman may be important but it does not involve the totality of the self. Only a very small part of me is the repairman.

Another way of describing the self-creating, spirit-constituting choice is to call attention to the subjective state of the person making it—"passion." A permanent choice, a total commitment of the self, a choice with passion, these constitute the person. No one choice is evidently right and all others wrong for a person, so it is not so much a question of what is chosen for the self but the earnestness, indeed the passion, with which one chooses. There is a strong correlation between spirit and passion. The person without passion is more likely to be determined by outside circumstances. He or she is less likely ever to choose definitely or ever to constitute a self. Rather than being an enemy of ethics, passion is a necessary condition for ethical existence.

Although the difference is not always discernible, we can often see it in a person who commits himself and one who does not. The person who is totally involved with the object of his choice can be seen to be a different person from the one who is not so committed, or is just partially there. We talk about certain tasks as vocations because they require total commitment. Many tasks can be vocationlike. The professions are just the easiest examples to identify—the priestly vocation or the medical vocation or the teaching vocation. Many craftsmen commit themselves totally to their work. They choose themselves as this or that definitively, and thereby create a self. Such persons have a distinctive personality—because their personality has been consolidated by their commitment. Others just work, and are whatever the circumstance seems to require them to be. If this latter type ever made a passionate and total commitment, the self thereby created would be distinct from the former self. It would not be a creation in the way God creates (out of nothing).

Much of the former being remains, especially the physical part. But on the other hand everything is changed. In this sense, choice is self-creating.

The chosen self has a history. Throughout the many changes in life, there is something which endures and which makes it possible to talk of this person's history. Things, events, moments are held together by his identity. These external facts are given form by this identity. Nothing is relinquished, not even that which is most fearful or hardest to bear. The very moments of time are lived through differently. Rather than the self being lost in each instant, the self has an enduring identity. There are on the other hand people without history, who do not know who they are, or have difficulty recognizing themselves at other times in their life. Self-choice gives structure and solidity to the self and makes it possible to build a life and then record its history.

For the human person it is not what he decides for his self or his life that counts but that such a decision is made. It is the choice of a certain self and not the object of the choice which makes the human person. The human person is constituted by a subjective act and not by those external aspects of the person which can be measured. This is not to say that the outside—the world, the environment is unimportant, but rather that it is not the essential determinant. A man without will to choose a certain concrete self does not become a self. Such a man will be controlled by external stimuli—or the surrounding environment, because he is nothing more than physical. The spirit comes to be in an act of the will, specifically the act of self-choice, and only spirit is more than the physical or capable of resisting the pressure of the physical. Spirit, freedom, self-choice—these are of the essence of the human person.

I may choose to be a parent, an international spy, or a priest. In any case I choose myself. I, who am an active relationship with myself, become person by an ethical choice in the sense of a choice of a certain type of self. Ethics is an inescapable aspect of human existence because man *must* respond to his own self. He *must* make a choice which is creative of the self and in so doing he posits the value of good. Self-choice is the very core of ethics as it is the core of man's spirituality. Ethics first and foremost is a concern with the self who actively responds. Only secondarily is it a concern with specific acts or behaviors. When man realizes his freedom in relationship to himself, then and only then does he become person and spirit.

Since self-choice creates a self, the absence of self-choice constitutes a radical human deficiency. Refusal to choose a certain self means that the person lacks identity, permanence, continuity. Self-choice unifies the self by giving it character and without self-choice no character develops. Who is he—or she? No one in particular. Today one thing, tomorrow another. The person loses himself in every involvement because there is no permanent identity or character which goes before and remains after the involvement. We are all familiar with the chameleon who is whatever is expected of him, or whatever will bring him "success."

Kierkegaard calls this type an aesthete and he uses this term to point up the importance of pleasure or wealth or power in such an existence. Given the absence of a center around which existence is ordered, life literally loses itself in every passing pleasure and in every passing fancy. There is nothing in such an existence to offer resistance to the flux of succeeding instants. Life is a variety of experiences determined by outside conditions. The joys, pleasures, satisfactions of the instant are all that exists. No permanent self (chosen self) precedes or succeeds the moment. The aesthete never chooses irretractably or permanently and consequently never unifies his own consciousness. He relates to and chooses always something outside the self: an object, a pleasure, an image. He never makes a definitive commitment of himself. The end result is diminished human existence. The self-relatedness that man essentially is never occurs. The self that *is to be created* never comes to be.

Because such an existence represents a radical deficiency it manifests itself in suffering. The young man or woman might seem perfectly satisfied with such an existence but as time goes by, *the lack* begins to be felt. The young person who refuses to relate to himself in any definitive way on the surface might seem to live an ideal existence. Never getting too deeply involved, he or she is free to change at any time. Because no permanent self has been chosen he or she can look forward to being anyone or anything. The aesthete is *free* with the freedom of the movie character "Alfie" who refuses even to choose permanently. He refuses to "settle down," or to limit himself to being one person. Nothing is excluded. Everything is possible.

If man is spirit in the sense of self-relatedness then the aesthete lacks spirit. He suffers from an absence of what man is essentially. To be human is to be self-assertive. Self-assertiveness, or self-choice, creates a center, without which the self is lost in every transitory satisfaction. Gradually this loss shows itself in a peculiar type of melancholy which overcomes the "free and frivolous" dilettante. Alfie suffered melancholy. We see basically the same type of person portrayed in opera, theater, novels, and plastic art. A strong anxiety infects the soul of the aging playboy or playgirl. There was a certain sadness, for example, which surrounded Nero even in the midst of his orgies. Nero, even more than Alfie, refused any permanent commitment and any binding responsibility. Everything was possible, because no limited finite self had been accepted. Nero tried to be God. In fact, he never became a human self and consequently was filled with melancholy and afraid even of little children.

The end of an existence that refuses to activate the self-relatedness which characterizes the human is despair. The power of choice, which man is, must be exercised in relation to himself or else man's very being is frustrated. Refusing to choose a self amounts to a refusal to be a person. Not becoming spirit creates a vacuum within man. This particular nonbeing or evil manifests itself emotionally in the cancers of melancholy and despair. Despair follows a refusal on the part of man to be "himself."

Despair is always about oneself, and the only way out of despair is choice. Man is a relatedness not primarily to the world but to himself, and the self that constitutes the human task is created only by a definitive self-choice. To relate to oneself is to choose oneself—and this is the most radical form of human freedom. Decision constitutes spirit because man is freedom. The man without will is radically flawed. Authentic man is an ethical being. He is free and called to exercise this freedom not just by choosing this or that thing in the world or by choosing this or that temporary involvement. Radical human freedom calls for actualization by the choice of an involvement which requires the whole of one's being, a total and absolute commitment. This type of self-choosing is not done once and for all, but is a task which requires constant renewal of choice. Because man is such a being we are justified in calling him ethical. It is an ethical choice (of a self) that constitutes the human person and this first or most radical ethical event is the foundation of ethics in the sense of a system of oughts and responsibilities.

Ordinarily ethics refers to specific acts: killing, abortion, adultery, stealing. There is, however, something more basic than an ethics of acts and that is an ethics of man's very being. Specific prescriptions for behavior are not the whole of ethics or even its most important concern. Good or bad acts are always so in relationship to *being*. What fulfills being is good; what diminishes or destroys being is bad. The choice of a certain self or type of being is fundamentally ethical because it constitutes the very ground of ethics. The choice of a certain self creates the foundation for what is of value. The self-choice is the ground not only of what is good and should be done but also of how it should be done. It is equally the ground of evil. What is to be done and what is to be avoided is precisely what contributes to the fulfillment of the self, chosen as doctor, or mother, or priest. The values emerge from the *being* of the person. What consolidates the personality, permeates and underlies its acts, is more fundamentally ethical than the acts of the person.

When a human being makes the fundamental ethical choice to become a certain type of person (to be a priest or to be married, to be a teacher or a mother, to go into music or to give one's life over to building a financial empire) immediately a whole series of duties begins to emerge. By willing ourselves as such and such, we *will* at the same time a set of standards associated with that type of life. Self-choice includes the choice of a system of values and rules. First it fixes the human self in a finite way (if I am a businessman I cannot be a doctor). Then it places the self in a context of the ethical obligation and responsibility associated with motherhood, business, medicine, etc. At the same time that the self is created, a set of standards emerges which the person chooses to live up to, as such and such a person. The objective content of the standards might come from Scripture, or from society, or even from myself (in the case in which I decide for myself the rules governing successful accomplishment of my chosen vocation). The important point is that the standards are chosen. I take responsibilities upon myself when I give my life a definitive direction by a self-constituting choice.

Here we pick up the line of reasoning with which we began this section. The responsibilities and duties which I assume in my free choice of a self, I gradually but very clearly recognize as the standards of negative judgment on myself. In other words, as I go about my chosen life, I constantly fail to live up to the values I freely chose to realize. I see myself as an ethical failure. I do not live up to my own ideals. I fall from my own standards. The experience of my life is such that I am forced to admit that I cannot be faithful to the claims of ethics, whatever their source or content. My conscience, if it is permitted to function, accuses me.

If a person's conscience is not just alive but sensitive, he or she will gradually come into a second type of despair—despair of the ethical. In other words, the human person who becomes a self, a spirit, a person, by accomplishing one task (that of activating the human self through self-relatedness) very soon finds himself in a new and different crisis. Sin, personal moral evil, comes into being after the innocence of youth is broken by a serious commitment. Sin is possible only for spirit, i.e., the self that has already limited itself to a determined direction and a specific set of values. Nevertheless, sin is part of every mature human existence and it is accompanied by a peculiar form of psychic discomfort called guilt. Worst of all, sin and guilt, despite our best efforts, abide with us. We never become what we choose to be. The attempt of modern psychotherapy to eliminate sin and guilt from human life is a mutilation of man because there is nothing more human than a sense of deficiency on the part of a person who is mature enough to have taken on responsibilities and dedicated himself to certain ideals. Guilt is not something pathological (although there are pathological forms of guilt), and the challenge is to handle it properly rather than eliminate it. Consciousness of guilt which follows morally defective behavior is a core human experience, the analysis of which will have a great deal to do with whether or not a person chooses for or against God.

Personal evil or sin is one of those unique and crucial human experiences which demand interpretation and response. One might see in this experience a pointer to God. As in other experiences we have examined, the opposite interpretation is also possible. Evil of any sort constitutes a problem for belief, and personal evil or sin is no exception. The atheist reacts by asking how a good God could permit sin and all the suffering it causes. It is also characteristic of atheism to interpret "sinfulness" in terms of determinants beyond personal control: e.g., instinct, or society, or lack of competence, or the demands of the situation. If sin or guilt is not successfully "explained away," then it is considered pathological. When faced with "sinful" behavior atheism adopts a version of "the devil made me do it" psychology, the devil being either an evil (capitalistic) society, or instinct, or the force of some external stimuli. Another possibility is to assume an *amoral* attitude and face behavior uncritically—"Well, that's just the way it is." Time and again atheism manifests itself as an acceptance of things as they are. It is a refusal to "go beyond" (transcendence) in the sense of seeing in any experience a pointer to "something more."

A theistic interpretation moves in the opposite direction. Sin and guilt are not reduced to something else or explained away but are seen as important and crucial human experiences. The human person in the course of development moves into responsibilities which he does not live up to and he realizes it. Human beings are conscious of their sin and conscious of an inability to rid themselves of sin. The moral weakness of human beings may be alleviated but never completely cured. In a person sensitive to his behavior, there is realization of ineradicable deficiency

directly related to acts or failures to act. He realizes that his
personal deficiencies are not the result of something external to
him, like limited capability, but of a failure to do what he was
perfectly capable of doing. Everyone is aware of having limited
capabilities and just as aware of the difference between such
limitations and actions or failures to act in the order of one's
vocational responsibilities which constitute serious personal
failure. Man falls not just from some objective standards imposed by an alien system of beliefs or an unchosen superego,
but from the very standards which the person chose for himself.
This leads to a new type of melancholy. The refusal to choose a
self definitively leads to melancholy and despair. Overcoming
this despair through choice and commitment, however, is not a
final overcoming. Melancholy and despair reenter human experience, now as accompaniments of recurring sin and consciousness of guilt.

Self-choice is aimed at the realization of a certain self and the
values associated with that self. Conscious acceptance makes
objective standards into personal values. The original self-
choice makes possible renunciation of or at least resistance to
the physical in favor of value. As life goes on, however, the
autonomous realization of values becomes more difficult, and
ultimately impossible. This is the foundation of guilt. It is not
guilt caused by this or that particular act but a much more
radical guilt, caused by the realization that we have not become
the person we had intended and aspired to. This guilt is a nos-
talgic regret of our very being.

There is another crisis that develops in human existence
when, usually around forty years of age, the person who committed himself to a certain existence (and gave himself an identity and a direction) gradually begins to realize that he or she
will never be the best mother, doctor, judge, priest, businessman, etc. The original choice of a self introduced a sense of
limit (if I'm a businessman, I cannot be a medical doctor, or if
I'm a mother, I cannot be a traveling dancer). Some years later
an even more radical sense of limit is introduced. Now the
person senses the limit imposed by his own failures. The failures
accumulate so that at age forty or forty-five or fifty, I have to

face the facts; I am not the mother I could have been, I am a mediocre doctor, etc. I have to face my failure—not the failure to be the *best*, which is obviously not a matter of personal responsibility, but the failure to be what I was very capable of being and in fact chose to be. In other words, I have to face my sins. Gradually human life slips into a second melancholy and a second despair.

This very situation poses fundamental questions about the human person. What is the nature of human existence? Shall I just accept this second type of despair? Is the challenge of life to grit one's teeth and bite the bullet in the sense of just accepting the "fact" that "this is the way it is"? Is human life, by reason of its essential structure of self-relatedness, a built-in tragedy in the sense that ultimately it requires choosing the self in sin, failure, guilt, melancholy, and finally despair? Does life so experienced have no exit? Is life structurally closed in on itself or is this a diabolic distortion of life's real structure? Or does the very structure of human existence open up to still another possibility? Must every man finally choose between being shut in and unfree or opened up and free for God?

The experience of evil we have been describing can be interpreted as a pointer to God. The God who is suggested by this aspect of human existence is not the God of hope, or the God of understanding, but a merciful and forgiving God. Either human life moves out of the experience of evil in the sense of sin and guilt into a relationship with God who forgives, or human life remains in guilt and despair.

Is human existence a programmed suffering or is there in the very experience of evil, sin, guilt, and the corresponding suffering a pointer to what might overcome the pain? What is the end of human life? Are we born so that we might come to sorrow, failure, sin, melancholy, guilt, and despair? Or is there in the evil, guilt, and despair a hidden good? Do sin and guilt and melancholy and despair actually prepare the human person for full humanness? Do these experiences not force still another choice of the self? Now the choice is narrowed to *the* crucial choice. Either I choose myself as I am, i.e., I choose myself in sin and guilt and despair and say that's all there is (atheism); or

I *interpret* the experience of a sinful, guilty, and despairing self as pointing beyond the self to God, the creator of the self who reveals himself to man in the experience of man's moral evil. In the latter case guilt reveals an even deeper aspect of human being. Guilt and deficient being suggest the opposite—being which is beyond guilt and deficiency. The experience of guilt and personal failure is not the only road to God, but it is a very often-traveled one. Man's final choice is to commit himself to God's mercy or to choose himself definitively as separate from God.

If this analysis of human experience is correct, then atheism is a choice of self as it is, i.e., the self which recognizes its deficiencies, and chooses itself as such. This is a heroic atheism which faces up to the human condition, and chooses it rather than taking refuge in some excuse for sin and guilt. Such atheism is a choice of the self in guilt and despair. It is a refusal to see in the experience of guilt a pointer to something else and at the same time a refusal to escape into some flimsy economic or psychological excuse for failure. The key to atheism is the phrase "that's the way life is—face it." It is heroic because to choose the self in despair is to look at the worst experience of life and accept it as final. That takes an uncommon courage, which is why there are so few real atheists.

Theism on the other hand is a refusal to accept the self in guilt and despair as final. It is a belief that human experience points to something beyond itself. Theism is a choosing of self or a self-relatedness in an extended sense, which includes the self as related to God as its creator. For theism, I am guilty and sinful but that is not all. There is "more," in that my sinful human self points to a forgiving creator to whom I am related. My guilt and sin point to him in relationship to whom sin and guilt are comprehensible. The limits of my being point to him who is without such limits; creature to creator, sinful to sinless, guilty to a being without guilt and yet forgiving. The first choice of the self as this or that person leads to a second choice as related or unrelated to God, pointed to by a more mature experience with life. The second choice, if made, embraces the self both as created and as needing redemption.

True religion is a choice of the self as related to God, creator and redeemer. It chooses the whole self. It refuses to close down on the self and shut the self off from help. Evil, in the sense of personal evil or sin, on the one hand, causes disbelief. (Many believing Jews lost their faith in the face of Nazi evil.) On the other hand, evil as the experience of one's own sinfulness places man in a situation which *can* suggest the existence of God as savior. Either God is and offers us forgiveness and salvation, or man is trapped, by the structure of his existence, in despair.

Religious faith in the sense of choosing oneself as related to God or as handing oneself over in relationship to God as savior is one response to the human situation we have been describing. Sin can lead to God. By admitting his faults man witnesses to his essential limitation before God. In choosing himself as so related man chooses his deepest self, which in fact is a gift and has a giver. Contrition or repentance does not change man into a saint, but it does remove the finality of guilt and despair. The choice of the self in repentance then is a choice of the deepest and fullest self, the self as related to God. Such a choice like the first self-choice is creative. In this second instance the choice of the self as related to God creates the religious self. It introduces the moment of eternity into the human condition.

As a matter of fact, the Scriptures contain many references to persons who move into a religious faith from an awareness of their sin. It is David's immorality that leads him to God. Many of his psalms are poetic pleas for forgiveness. And David is not an isolated example. On the other hand, the same Scriptures contain other interpretations of and reactions to the same experiences. There is the repeated warning against hardness of heart. That phrase for the Jew meant something very much like what we have been trying to describe with the language of choosing despair. If we look to Scripture as a privileged perspective on human experience we find countless examples of what we have been describing as the second choice of the self, or the choice of the whole self which includes the self as creature. Sin, awareness of personal deficiency, and guilt constitute a revelation. Man moves to God only after seeing himself as he is. Hardness of heart or refusal to see is a Scriptural description of atheism. "Soft-heartedness" in the sense of sensitivity to one's personal failures and "seeing" this experience as pointing beyond itself is in Scripture a grace or a gift.

Paradoxically, sin both separates man from God and is a primordial human experience which reveals man's relationship to God. David's religiosity is a good example of how sin reveals both man's creaturehood and God's transcendence. Without such a revelation no true relationship with God is possible. We are trying to suggest that the experience of sin or personal evil is a critical and altogether normal human experience that might be interpreted as pointing to God. The message of Scripture is similar but stronger. In Scripture sin actually reveals God; conscious sin is already a relationship with God; man is fully himself only in his choice of God as savior.

Love and God

A great deal was said in Part 2 on the nature of human love and its place in authentic human life. Here a slightly different question is asked. While presuming the central place of love in human life we inquire whether the experience of love is religiously significant. Is there anything about either the positive experience of loving or the negative experience of the absence of love which can serve as the beginning of a religious reflection? Is love a pointer to something more? Is there a *someone* more, who created man a loving being and is the ultimate fulfillment of his need for love?

One influential thinker who answered this question in the affirmative was Plato. It is hardly necessary to comment on Plato's stature. Suffice it to say that Whitehead, the great American thinker, held that all Western philosophy was a commentary or a footnote to Plato. The great Greek master treated the topic of love in many places (in the *Apology, Lysis, Gorgias, Phaedo, Republic, Timaeus, Laws*). The most famous treatment, however, appeared in the *Symposium* and we will use that statement to offer an example of love reflected upon and interpreted as pointing to God.

Everywhere in Greek philosophy there is concern for human happiness. Both Plato and Aristotle use that word (*eudaimonia*, translated into English by *happiness*) to refer to what we might call fulfillment, perfection, the making of our human being a work of art. Happiness in this sense is the end or goal of human life. Love plays a crucial role in human happiness because it is that which drives man toward those things which are for his fulfillment.

Love in Plato is a force or a drive or a surge toward union with what fulfills man and consequently fills him with joy. The drama of human life unfolds around love. Man must learn to avoid false goods which lead to corruption and death. Only by loving and uniting with what is truly good can man fulfill himself. If man loves, pursues, and unites with the good and the beautiful his life will be happy. If he loves, pursues, and unites with the unworthy his life will be lost. The key to life is knowing what to love.

Plato's outline of the proper objects of love includes, in the highest place, the supreme good. Life, then, if it be fulfilled, must end up in a passionate pursuit of what is beyond this world or beyond the physical. While love takes its first steps in what we might call sexual love of another person, it must move beyond that experience to the pursuit of and finally union with ever higher goods. Ultimately love unites the truly happy man with supreme goodness, supreme beauty, and the highest excellence.

According, then, to Plato's theory, love cannot be identified with frenzied and irrational sexual passion. Nor is it a fear which paralyzes the mind and drives the enchanted one to madness or death. Rather the opposite is true. Plato's concept of love starts at the opposite pole from the romantic image of love. In Plato, love is urge, and desire, but not divorced from reason. Love and rationality in Plato are joined. Loving is actually a clearer way of "seeing" or perceiving "the way things really are." Love extends beyond sexual desire for another person to desire for all those goods which are for man's well-being. The distinction between true and false love depends upon the object loved. True love is pursuit and union with that which leads to fulfillment. False love is always mixed with irrationality or stupidity and pursues what is in no way conducive to human fulfillment. Tragedy comes from loving the wrong things. The human life in Plato's thought which does not gradually come to *understand* that man's fulfillment lies in loving and pursuing spiritual rather than material values misses the point of life.

Love then for Plato includes insight or intelligence. It is not sufficient to be a lover in the sense of being able to feel attraction and desire. True love must include an *awareness* of what is finally desirable and what is not worthy of man's pursuit. We can then judge the quality of a man by looking at what he loves. The lover of money, food, applause, or a fleeting pleasure is a lover with flawed intelligence. True love, permeated by insight and rationality, knows what is truly beautiful, and for man's happiness. True love is desire for *the* good. The good is what contributes to man's fulfillment. The crucial problem is to discern the genuine good from the fake goods which appear desirable but do not bring man happiness.

There is in Plato no Puritanism or flight from sexuality. He does not shy away from the sexual aspects of human love relations but interprets them as the beginning of a broader, life-fulfilling project. *The* most important drive or desire in life is love. For him, however, it is the root of every human pursuit and is not confined to erotic relationships. Sexual love according to Freud is the fundamental need, to which all other needs can be reduced. For Plato sexual love is only one manifestation of a much broader desire in man for fulfillment or happiness. While Freud tries to see in all manner of human desire a camouflaged form of sex, Plato sees in sex an important indication of human desire. It is, according to Plato, not pleasure pure and simple, but fulfillment which man pursues. Love drives man toward growth and human perfection which finally comes through a union with the highest good.

Sexual love, and the generation of children, is, then, an elementary effort at something far more important. Sexual love is real love but an experience which opens itself to further analysis. It is a "pointer to something more." Sexual love is creative but not in the fullest sense of human creativity. Man is capable of even more satisfying creations than sex. It is the tragic man who through blindness holds himself to nothing beyond sexual satisfaction or having children. What is today called "sexual liberation" and enlightenment, for Plato is short-sightedness and slavery. Were he living today he would accuse us of seeing only the surface of things and missing the deeper levels of reality. Our concentration on sex would in his judgment cover up an inability to understand the real significance of sexual love. He would accuse the sexual "avant garde" of stupidity.

Falling in love makes everything more beautiful. The whole world unlocks its secrets to the lover. The reality of the person loved, his true inner qualities, are revealed. Love brings a heightened awareness, a greater clarity, a more realistic vision of the world. This is, however, just a beginning. The next step is an awareness of more spiritual forms of beauty. Physical love leads to a desire for union with more spiritual forms of goodness and beauty. It opens our eyes to deeper levels of reality. Love quickens both intelligence and a capacity for union. The lover moves from physical love of another person to desire for union of the self with goodness and beauty in the form of justice, wisdom, courage (spiritual goods). "Platonic love" then is not love without sexuality but love which moves from sexuality to spirituality. Love begins in sex and ends in mysticism and union with the highest spiritual reality. It is not tragic that a person's desire is generated by some lower object—money, or power, or sexual satisfaction. The human person, however, cannot be fulfilled in love that terminates here. Fulfillment is spiritual growth, deep satisfaction, and finally victory over death, all of which come from loving the supreme good.

Caution is required in the identification of Plato's *supreme good* or *the form of the Good* and God as ordinarily understood. God is for us a *conscious person*, creator, judge, etc. Plato's supreme form is *not* personal and exercises none of the usual functions of the Judeo-Christian God. But there are obvious parallels between Plato's supreme good and our concept of God. Both are supreme, spiritual, ultimate, absolute, and beyond conceptual categorization. While Plato does not always give religious qualities to the Good, there is a strong religious tone to Plato's philosophy which stands out clearly in certain works. The Idea of the Good has a markedly religious character in the *Republic*. In the *Symposium* the very same atmosphere is evident. The Good becomes God as ordinarily understood and human life is interpreted as a drive toward God. Augustine's line, "Our hearts were made for Thee, O Lord, and shall not rest until they rest in Thee," is not alien to the spirit we find in Plato's *Symposium*.

Plato, then, interprets human love as a surge or drive toward union with what brings happiness. Complete happiness can come only when human love leads to a union with God. Man then for Plato is a drive for fulfillment in God. His view of man can be compared with that of Augustine, Aquinas, Dante, St. Theresa of Avila, and others, for whom human love, if fully developed, unites the person with God enjoyed in a mystical rapture. Love for Freud is reduced to sex. His judgment can be characterized as "That's all there is." Plato and all the other above-mentioned thinkers see in the experience of love a pointer beyond itself to "something more."

In the *Symposium* Plato asks, through the person of Socrates, whether love itself is God. He answers in the negative. Love rather, he says, is a *daemon*—a spirit, which binds heaven and earth. "For God mingles not with man, but through love all the intercourse and converse of God with man, whether awake or asleep, is carried on."[1] Love then not only binds man with woman in the ecstasy of sexual love, but is a symbol of an ever more substantial fulfillment: the ecstasy of union between man and God.

Hegel is another philosophical giant who addressed himself to the question of love. Hegel's stature as a philosopher makes it possible to compare him with Plato. He developed the greatest synthesis of knowledge known to modern man. His work

---

1. Plato, "Symposium," *The Dialogues of Plato*, 3rd ed., trans. Benjamin Jowett (New York and London: Oxford University Press, 1892), 1:572.

covered practically every field. Not only did he analyze each but he tried to show the laws of development and their interrelationship. A great deal of contemporary philosophy is indebted to Hegel. Marxism is Hegelian philosophy with a strong dose of French economics. Existentialism is a commentary on Hegel. Even American and British philosophy have been decisively influenced by him.

Our interest is in Hegel's philosophy of human nature. For Hegel all reality is spirit and man is spirit developed to the stage of self-consciousness. An analysis of the human then for Hegel is an analysis of man's peculiar and highly developed form of consciousness. Correspondingly for Hegel the search for man's essence is a search for the structure of genuine reality. Since everything is fundamentally spirit at some stage of development, the human, which is highly developed spirit, becomes the key to understanding everything else. The proper study of man then is a study of mind or spirit or consciousness. Love, if it is important for human life, will have to be a function of human consciousness.

Consciousness begins (in the small baby) in a state of unity with everything else. For the baby, there is only one reality. Everything is one for the infant consciousness. Here there are no oppositions—no separateness. Hegel uses the term *immature consciousness* to refer to this primary and primitive stage. It is, however, important to note that unity and oneness characterize this beginning phase of consciousness' voyage because maturity will be a creative recovery of this blissful beginning.

As consciousness develops, through the acquisition of language, it becomes separate or set apart from things which it is not. Gradually the child learns words for chair, table, Mommy, etc., and so becomes *conscious* of his or her own separateness from these. *Objects* emerge in that they are separate from consciousness. Consciousness is no longer one with everything but over and against everything. Everything else becomes an *object* for consciousness (the subject).

For Hegel alienation or separateness is necessary for the development of mind. Without gradually developing opposition between the individual consciousness and all else there is no progress. It is this separation of the conscious self from other people and other things that makes possible *objective* awareness, analysis, scientific understanding. Consciousness requires an objectivity. Because of separateness, objective knowledge is possible and paradoxically also subjective knowledge. The subject comes to understand himself or herself through relationships set up by the separation. Man's mind (man himself) develops in a dialectical struggle with everything that he is not.

Some of Hegel's most famous pages were written about the dialectical relationship between the self (the subject or the individual consciousness) and the other (in the sense of the other human being). Each conscious being finds out who and what he is in a struggle with other consciousnesses. In his well-known master-slave analogy, Hegel showed that one form this struggle takes is domination. Some human beings handle the problems generated by their separateness from others by dominating the other. In such a case the master is as mutually dependent upon the slave as the slave is upon the master. Both are unhappy or alienated forms of consciousness. Originally the master seems to be successful and happy but this is short-lived. The master is less fearful than the slave, less concerned with saving his life, but he gradually becomes enslaved by his dependence on the slave. The original slave—the weaker, more fearful consciousness, through his labor, imprints his self upon nature and thereby comes to be self-determined and dominant. Because the master-slave relationship is not the proper solution to the problem of each man's separateness it ends up with unhappiness for both parties.

The proper solution—the only solution that will bring the individual consciousness from unhappiness to fulfillment—is the relationship of love. The seed of consciousness begins in unity, grows through oppositions, and finally comes to happiness through a recovery of the original unity in love. Love for Hegel is required by the very structure of human consciousness. It is a necessity built into the essence of man. Universally, human beings value love because their nature is such that love is the key to fulfillment. The separateness which man experiences is necessary for his development but it is also a source of pain and anxiety. Loneliness is the worst form of suffering. Love on the other hand is the greatest delight because it overcomes separateness without destroying the development associated with separateness. Love unites individuals without destroying the particular or subsuming one consciousness into the other.

> [In love] life has run through the circle of development from an immature to a completely mature unity: when the unity was immature, there still stood over against it the world and the possibility of a cleavage between itself and the world; as development proceeded, reflection produced more and more oppositions (unified by satisfied impulses) until it set the whole of man's life in opposition [to objectivity]; finally, love completely destroys objectivity and thereby annuls and transcends reflection, deprives man's opposite of all foreign character, and discovers life itself without any further defect. In love the separate does still remain, but as something united and no longer as something separate; life [in the subject] senses life [in the object].[1]

Man then is man only insofar as he is in relationship with other self-consciousnesses. Isolation or loneliness is a destructive curse. Domination is a form of isolation and correspondingly dehumanizing. Individualism which emphasizes separateness condemns to immaturity. Full human maturity takes place only in that form of togetherness men call love. To view others as set off over and against the self, or to view oneself as set off and separate, is to fail to understand the structure of the human. The essence of man requires that the human person transcend his individuality or separateness in a loving union with others. Without love man will not come to be what he is. He will fail to be himself. He will be a tragic animal.

What does all this have to do with God? Is there anything in this analysis of man's essence which might be seen from the perspective of religion? Hegel thought so. For him, it was not a coincidence or an accident that the revelation of God in Jesus

---

1. G. W. F. Hegel, "Love," in *Early Theological Writings*, tr. by T. M. Knox (Philadelphia: University of Pennsylvania Press, 1971), p. 305.

coincides with what rational analysis reveals about human nature. Hegel saw the history of man as a history of failure to come to grips with the demands of love. Men emphasized and institutionalized their individuality, their separateness, and their isolation from one another. These failures explain God's intervention into human history to save man. The only hope for mankind is in the solution which Jesus taught or which God revealed in Jesus. The love which will save man is God's love— i.e., the love made possible by God communicating his own life to us. Universal love, required by man's essence, points to the revelation of God in Jesus Christ. There is a correlation between man's structure and God's revelation.

> To love God is to feel one's self in the "all" of life, with no restrictions, in the infinite. In this feeling of harmony there is no universality, since in a harmony the particular is not in discord but in concord, or otherwise there would be no harmony. "Love thy neighbor as thyself" does not mean to love him as much as yourself, for self-love is a word without meaning. It means "love him as the man whom thou art," i.e., love is a sensing of a life similar to one's own, not a stronger or a weaker one. Only through love is the might of objectivity broken, for love upsets its whole sphere.[1]

If there is more than a coincidence between the nature of man and God's invitation to loving relationship with him, then our secular age would have to be humanly deficient. Both Plato and Hegel argue that love is required by the very structure of human existence and that religion or a loving relation with God is the natural direction of human development. The absence of religion in a culture would show up as an absence of what is required for full humanness. If they are right we would expect problems with love in a purely secular society like our own. Evidence that this is in fact the case is not hard to come by. On the one hand in our society love is held up as salvation. "All

---

1. *Ibid.*, p. 247.

you need is love." Those who find love are as self-confident about success as a Calvinist who accumulates a fortune. On the other hand, however, hard statistical data (e.g., divorce rates) show that successful love is more and more *un*common. Some thinkers, arguing from the way things are to the way they have to be, insist that love is an impossibility (Sartre and Laing).

The crisis of love in our time is most clearly reflected in our art. The artist lives out the consciousness of his age with greater sensitivity than the ordinary person and he expresses the struggles others only dimly perceive. Our dramatists, for example, present one shocking play after another in which personal communication of even a minimal sort is absent. There is no love in the tragic characters of Ionesco, Genet, Beckett, Pinter, Osborne. Osborne and Genet show us how violence has become a substitute for love. Beckett, Pinter, and Ionesco show us characters who cannot communicate (e.g., in *Krapp's Last Tape,* Krapp relates only to himself through the medium of a tape recorder). The message, repeated over and over in one form or another, is that contemporary man is an isolated, separated consciousness. He is a tragic figure without love.

For those who prefer movies just as many examples could be listed. Analyze *Midnight Cowboy, Alfie, Last Tango in Paris,* and the same theme surfaces. Or look at the popularity of films which substitute violence for love. The whole scene adds up to a convincing portrait of contemporary man as a being who is in trouble because of a failure of love. Contemporary man seeks for love in the easiest form, i.e., sex. Time and again he winds up disappointed. The midnight cowboy tried pure sex and was "saved" from total destruction by a homosexual relationship with a pitiful character played by Dustin Hoffman. Hoffman reminds us of *The Graduate.* Again we have a story about a search for love, the unsatisfactoriness of pure, physical sex, the leap to a marriage which we are left suspecting will never work. *Alfie* too is a man who wants sexual love but without commitment (the *Playboy* ideal). He winds up condemned to his own selfish isolation. ("What's it all about, Alfie?") Brando in *Last Tango* masterfully portrays the "aging" contemporary man who, faced with death, seeks salvation in pure physical sex. He

are suffering from a loss of openness to one another. He might agree that *evil* is separateness, isolation, swollen impersonalness. And yet he might conclude, "That's the way it is." The suggestion that these experiences can be interpreted as pointing to an absent God or lost religion rests upon an anterior presupposition that these human experiences point beyond themselves. Rather than just being what they are and nothing more, these experiences are presumed to be something deeper. They have to be seen as bearing meaning or being pregnant with deeper significance. If they point to something more, then the more may very well be the God of Scripture. Why? Because this God is a *Thou* inviting man to real I-Thou relationship. If we have become *thingified* by valuing the impersonal over the personal, then we are not just losing the richness of person-to-person relationships but losing as well the saving wealth of a relationship with the Absolute Person.

As in the other sections, too, we are concentrating on evil and trying to move from an experience of evil to God. Secular man today tends to compartmentalize his existence. He works —that's the first thing. Work for contemporary man is separated from personal relationships and made a fully justifiable enterprise in itself. Because much of what he does is sterile and impersonal and meaningless, he needs longer and longer periods of relief. At work profit is what counts, not people. Because work is so separated from human purposes and need, it exhausts man spiritually as well as physically. Other persons are used as means to ends in day-to-day business operations. Even the longer and longer periods of relief required by this type of work tend to be as impersonal as the work itself. Notice people today "enjoying themselves." Sex for many has become a relief from the tensions created by work rather than love making. Alcohol, which supposedly facilitates relationships, becomes a potion used to blot out the other and the world. All this amounts to evil because the core of human existence is relational, and warm, loving, caring, personal relationships are exactly what become suppressed in a lust for some*thing* else (power, money, status). Is it possible that "the way it is" is in fact *demonic*? Are people being destroyed by being drawn away from the core of human existence? Does this demonic evil point to this opposite? Does one side of the coin suggest the other? Does the demise of personal love (evil) in our experience point to the personal God who both reveals himself in love and makes love possible by communicating his own loving self?

People in our times run to the new cults of psychotherapy to find a cure for their illness. The scream therapists vie with the transactional analysts and behaviorists to help man find the other who has become lost. Sensitivity sessions, touch sessions, nude sessions are all designed to bring salvation from the hell of separateness and isolation. Mistrust and hostility are the evil spirits which occupy the space in man's life meant for love and warm encounter. He can no longer be direct and open and authentic with his fellow man. His contacts are stereotyped or carried on with masks because making an impression is good for business. Real conversation has become a rarity. Propaganda rules even in the private world. Man feels spiritually sick and looks for a cure.

Is there a possibility that the evil that man suffers actually is related to God, or better the absence of God? Can the whole contemporary scene be understood as a death of God? God is dead because man has become incapable of relationship. If God is person inviting to dialogue, then man, who has grown sick, can no longer hear the invitation. He finds it difficult to "imagine" what God or a relationship with God would be like. Images of God are born of encounters and he has lost the knack of meeting. If God is Person he will of necessity be hidden from those who make their lives with things. Perhaps the contemporary experience of man is best understood as an eclipse of God. If so, what is left for contemporary man caught in isolation and darkness? Perhaps he could start by doing what others have done in such situations. Cry out. "Our Father. . . ."

Concluding Postscript

The worst moment in the production of a book is the first moment. Facing that first blank page is a traumatic experience. Once the first steps are taken a writer can "fall into a pace" which carries him along. The productive process will never be smooth. There will be snags, fears of losing the thread, concerns about what to include or what to leave out, times of depression and exhaustion. But the work already done on a book acts as a continuing prod. It requires completion and makes its claim on the writer. Once begun then, the next most difficult decision is where to stop. How much material makes a book? Is there a recapitulation required? Is there one more point or so which should be made in order to tie up the package?

Anyone who has read to this point hardly needs to reread in order to catch the point. The three Parts are well defined. The survey of contemporary man's situation with special emphasis on the many new forms of alienation naturally raises a question about the nature of man. If man is alienated, then there must be some nature from which he has become estranged. The second Part outlines a fairly traditional philosophy of human nature. It attempts to show the constitutive characteristics of man's being along with the demands which each makes on him. The many forms of contemporary dissatisfaction and neurosis are the result of a culture which ignores the nature of human existence. Consequently there are many cases of persons mishandling the demands of their own natures. The first two Parts set the stage for the final question of whether man's nature includes a religious element. Is man, among other things, a capability for relationship with God? Does the proper handling of the demands of human existence require the actualization of his religious potential? Can contemporary man's cultural deficiencies be made somewhat more comprehensible by pointing up the absence of a religious dimension to contemporary civilization?

The attempt in the final section to suggest that an analysis of human experience points to the possibility of God is incomplete without a substantiation of man's interest in religion. Human experience might be shown to point to God, and still man might react by saying, so what? As a matter of fact, he does not, because he is a naturally religious animal. In the peak of animal evolution appears an ape who raises a question about the purpose of his existence. This question reflects a radically new form of consciousness. Because the question is constitutive rather than peripheral to human existence it is raised with burning intensity. It is the peculiar characteristic of the human ape that he questions with special interest the reason for his being and inquires about the quality of his existence. His questioning is more than curiosity. An answer is demanded. To question the purpose of existence, or to inquire about the conditions for the possibility of human life, is to ask about the existence of God. The God question then emerges from the very core of human being.

There are countless activities of human life which might upon reflection serve as pointers to God. Besides the experiences we tried to analyze from the religious perspective there are the emotions of joy, grief, desire, peace, apathy, ennui, disgust. Love we loked at, but there is also hate. Then there are the future-oriented experiences like hope, plans, aims, fidelity. We looked at reasoning and inquiring, but there is also imagination, fantasy, play, celebration. Man chooses and sometimes he chooses to deceive himself. Associated with self-deception are feelings of alarm, discomfort, bias, uncertainty, insecurity. What we were concerned with appear as critical or core experiences but this is so only from one perspective. Human experience spills over any attempt to organize it into a system and provides material sufficiently complex for eons of analyses. When time ends man will still be a mystery to himself and God will still be an option which can be embraced or rejected on the basis of differing interpretations of the human. The central drama continues, *usque ad finem*.

God is present to human beings in somewhat the same way that one personality is present to another. The character of the other person is present in a meeting with him. His character or deeper self expresses itself in his many words and gestures. And yet the deeper self is not immediately present. An interpretation is required in order to get at the deeper reality. Certain privileged actions and words give me access to both my own deeper self and that of others. They point to the reality behind the gestures or the word. The personality is revealed in these, if there is someone capable of making the interpretation and interested enough to carry out the task.

A claim by Jewish writers is made that God, whom man naturally inquires about, has revealed himself not only in human experience but also in the events of history. According to sacred Jewish literature God is present in certain mediating events much in the same way that personality is present in words and gestures. These become signs which point beyond. They require interpretation. Biblical personalities, especially the prophets, presumed to interpret the events of history as revelatory signs. They interpreted them not only as pointing to God, but as God's very words. "Thus sayeth the Lord."

The man in the street is never quite that certain about the presence of God. He asks the religious question. Certain personal experiences might point to the possibility of God. On the other hand, however, he finds himself plagued by gnawing doubts. Living in a secular and scientific culture creates many obstacles to religious belief. The culture predisposes a person not to believe. In addition it contributes to a weakening of religious questioning. A culture may stimulate the development of man's nature or it may repress and ultimately destroy some aspect of it. The typical product of our culture shows a distinct loss of interest in the God question which belongs naturally to human being.

Another way of expressing the same situation is to say that contemporary man's doubting is more than an exercise of critical intelligence. Doubting in the sense of being rationally cautious or critical can be and often is a force pushing man toward further inquiry. Contemporary secular man's doubt, however, is not a stimulus to further inquiry. He doubts with the whole of his existence and not just cognitively. His doubting takes the form of a lack of heart or interest in the whole affair of religion. His "heart is not in" the search for God. He does not pretend to be satisfied with his life but he resists embarking on a religious project or quest. He doubts—not in some abstract, rational sense—but with his whole person. He *feels* uncertain, distant, and alien from the whole world of organized religion. As a result religion has a great deal to overcome even to be considered as a real possibility—and correspondingly to generate *wholehearted interest*.

The alienation of contemporary man from religion certainly has its cognitive or rational element. There are intellectual doubts or doubts about the formal propositions of religion but these are not the major problem. Rather it is a deep estrangement he feels from religion which cannot be cured by purely intellectual argument. Contemporary man often feels radical dissatisfaction with his life. He would like to be inspired, to face life more energetically and from a perspective different from the one he has grown into. Vital purpose, inner strength, hope, these he would like, but religion as he knows it seems inappropriate to such aspirations, Consequently, secular man faces his life alone. Life is filled with suffering, disappointment, and evil. God, however, seems implausible. Organized religion seems either innocuous or evil. So in effect there is no *exit*—no salvation. Given this situation, an approach to the religious for contemporary man must be more than an intellectual exercise.

The classical arguments for the existence of God seem far removed from real life. It is difficult for us to identify with them or to be greatly moved by their logic for the simple reason that the logic is in no way rooted in our life experience. The classical arguments seem more like exercises in abstract thought process than instruments for moving a whole person toward a religious perspective. If an argument of any sort hopes to convince it must be consistent or logical or free from error. This, however, is not all that is required. Where a change in the whole person is aimed at, logical consistency alone is insufficient. Unless the elements of the argument can be rooted in one's personal experience, or be identified as part of a person's lived experience, he or she might be "rationally" convinced but never radically changed. "A change of heart" or a "turning" toward a different life perspective is a much more serious undertaking than just "changing one's mind."

Our approach to God has been something less than an attempt to prove in the sense of forcing one's intellectual assent. Rather we tried to analyze lived experience such that a religious possibility might emerge. If contemporary man can identify with the experience described and analyzed, then perhaps he can identify with the religious perspective suggested. Ours has been an approach to God which begins with the lived experience of man in the seventies. It assumes that the person who follows the description will still in the end have to take a risk in order to change his heart or become religious. Faith is never forced by either a "knock-down" proof or a "knock-down" analysis.

The leap to faith is not a blind one but it is always a jump that is preceded by anxiety. This is especially true of the Christian faith. The specifically different content of the Christian faith gives a special character to the trust and commitment associated with it. To believe that there is intention and purpose manifested in reality and that the source is in God, a personal being, qualifies a person as a religious believer. He or she might go on to believe that this personal God revealed himself in Jewish history and then in a special way through the life of a Jewish prophet named Jesus. These beliefs require a trust and a commitment which lead to a Christian style of life. Following Jesus, the religious believer tries to found his life on the virtue of love. If reality is fundamentally good and love is the key to good life, then the Christian must try to reach out in a healing, forgiving way toward those from whom he is separated. He trusts that this is the way life was meant to be. In addition he trusts that God, who revealed himself in Jesus, will act that way toward him, forgiving him and empowering him to begin again to love after failure.

The Christian faith has a strong personalistic dimension, not only because it is dedicated to the dignity of the individual person, but more importantly because it is faith in someone and not just some things. There are truths or faith statements which are held to be true but Christian faith is fundamentally a relationship to someone—the person Jesus Christ. The astronauts had faith "in the guys back in Houston" and this was strong enough to keep them together even when the scientific apparatus failed. There is a similar quality to Christian faith. Christian faith is different because it involves a real relationship to a person. Commitment to him and trust in him has its ups and downs in a Christian life but this reciprocal mutual interrelationship sets the Christian believer apart. We might say that the special content of Christianity is the person Jesus. Commitment to him produces a distinguishing life style.

The point of this book then narrows down to a fairly simple question. Can secular man bring himself to seriously reconsider the God question, or the Jesus question? If man is by nature a religious animal then a consideration of radical questions about human existence is part of being human. The person who has lost this religious curiosity has lost part of his humanness, and not just an interchangeable part. To experience one's human being is to feel the bite of the religious question. Man can push aside the inquiry. He can choose to repress the question. His culture might lead to a deadening of this aspect of his existence. If, however, he has retained the bite of human being he will feel pained in his alienated state. Contemporary man may have to make a hell of his existence before he comes around to consider an alternative.

Before the secularization process began, belief was both total and passionate. As we moved into our age of science, technology, and industrialization, belief became weakened. Unbelief not only became an acceptable alternative to religion but became in some places, as belief had once been, passionate and total. Belief and unbelief traded places. During the middle ages, no concession was made to doubt about God. Later societies grew up where no concession was made to doubt about atheism. In both cases, an awesome mechanism of repression was required. The Inquisition tried to kill off the reservations which developed within the religious belief system. Today political repression in Marxist societies teams up with subtler forms of scientific and positivistic pressures in capitalist countries to hold back the rumblings of suspicion about the possibility of God. The pressures not to believe today are in some places just as real as once were the pressures to believe.

Before a secular person can seriously reconsider religion or the Christian faith he might have to overcome considerable pressure from his culture. Besides the courage required for belief, trust, and commitment, there is an anterior courage required even to seriously consider the religious question. People today live in the first culture in man's whole history which has no God experience as its inspiration. To consider religion means going against the dominant cultural myths. Solzhenitsyn, for example, stood up against the Marxist myth and the Soviet system which had taken the lives of its first revolutionary heroes, eliminated millions of kulaks, imprisoned millions more ordinary citizens, and turned the lives of tens of millions into a hell. Westerners heartily agreed with his "revelations" of the Marxist system. He documented what "they knew all along."

It is, however, interesting how the other part of Solzhenitsyn's thesis is downplayed by Western commentators. Solzhenitsyn also accuses the secular capitalistic system and myth. He accuses both his own people and people in the West of an absence of morality and indifference to God. The Marxist press heaps abuse on him for both his religious faith and his criticism of the system. His religious faith for them is a pure proof that he is either soft-minded or crazy. His criticism of Marxist ideology is explained away by calling attention to all the money he has made on his books.

Western commentary tends simply to ignore the "other part" of the message. Solzhenitsyn's insistence that a God relationship belongs to the very structure of human existence and his linking widespread immorality to practical atheism is politely passed over. He is considered a hero for having the courage to make the political criticism but not for making the religious criticism. As a matter of fact, however, it took courage to make both witnesses and courage will be required to take his witness seriously. The courage which is required for every human person to affirm himself in the face of threats coming from the physical, spiritual, ethical, and social dimensions of his existence is not magically dispensed with when man faces the religious.

Index

Index